Kate Brownlee Sherwood

Campfire, Memorialday And Other Poems

Kate Brownlee Sherwood

Campfire, Memorialday And Other Poems

ISBN/EAN: 9783744713764

Printed in Europe, USA, Canada, Australia, Japan

Cover: Foto ©Thomas Meinert / pixelio.de

More available books at **www.hansebooks.com**

CAMP-FIRE, MEMORIAL-DAY,

AND

OTHER POEMS.

BY

KATE BROWNLEE SHERWOOD.

.

CHICAGO:

JANSEN, McCLURG, & COMPANY.

1885.

R. R. Donnelley & Sons, The Lakeside Press.

IN THE SPIRIT OF

FRATERNITY, CHARITY, AND LOYALTY,

TO WHOSE MAJESTIC MEASURES THE

VETERANS OF THE GRAND ARMY OF THE REPUBLIC

HAVE TIMED THEIR STEPS,

I BRING THESE SIMPLE RECITALS OF FEALTY AND VALOR

IN HONOR OF THE LIVING AND IN REVERENT MEMORY OF THE DEAD,

AND LAY THEM ON THE ALTAR OF

MY COUNTRY—REUNITED, REGENERATED,

AND AT PEACE.

CONTENTS.

PART I.

PART I.

——

CAMP-FIRE AND MEMORIAL-DAY POEMS.

MEMORIES OF THE WAR.

WHENEVER I hear the fife and the drum,
  And the bugle wildly play,
My heart is stirred like a frightened bird,
  And struggles to break away ;
For the tramp of the Volunteers I hear,
  And the Captain's sharp command :
"Left! Left! Left!"   He is near
  And drilling his eager band.

For the women and men were at one that day,
  In a purpose grand and great ;
But the men are away in a stormy fray,
  And the women must watch and wait.

And some were as brown as the tawny South,
  And some like the dawn were fair ;
And here was the lad with his girlish mouth,
  And there was the beard of care.
But whether from farm or from fold they drew,
  From the shop or the school-boy's seat,

9

Each shouldered his musket and donned the blue,
    And the time with his brogans beat.

And the mother put motherly fears to flight,
    And the wife hid her tears away ;
For men must fight when their cause is right,
    While the women in patience pray.

And now 'tis the discipline hard and sore
    Of the camp and the march and the chase,
And now 'tis the flash and the crash and the roar,
    As the battle creeps on apace.
O God ! it is hard when a comrade falls,
    With his head at your very feet,
While *"Forward!"* the voice of your Captain calls,
    And the enemy beats retreat.

And O for the mother or wife who must see,
    When the news of the battle is known :
"Killed, Private C. of Company G,"
    While she sits in her grief like stone.

Here, the pitiless siege and the hunger that mocks ;
    There, the hell of Resaca waits ;

And the crash of the shell on the Georgia rocks,
  As you beat on Atlanta's gates.
There are dreams of a peace that is slow to dawn,
  Of the furloughs that never come ;
There are tidings of grief from a letter drawn,
  And the silence of lips grown dumb.

The words of your messmate you write from the crag
  Where he breathed his life away :
" O say to my darling I died for the flag
  She blessed when we marched that day."

There are chevroned sleeves for some who may go,
  And a captain's straps for a few,
And the scars of the hero that some may show
  When is sounded the last tattoo ;
But the upturned face on the enemy's side,
  With its cold and ghastly stare,
Is all that is left of the pomp and the pride
  Of some who the conflict share.

And lo, when the enemy lifts the dead
  And rifles his breast, I ween

There's a woman's face and the dainty grace
 Of the babe he never has seen.

And O for the famine, and O for the woe,
 Of the comrades in prison pens !
For the hunger and thirst, and the fever slow,
 And the torturing homesick sense !
And O for the phantoms that walk by night
 And the phantoms that walk by day !
And the whirl of the brain in the hopeless fight
 With the demons that gloat and prey !

And O for the scenes that they loved so well,
 That haunted their dying day,—
For a draught from the well that will never swell,
 And a breath of the new-mown hay !

Ah well, there are few who are left, we know,
 Of the many who marched away ;
And the children who clung to our skirts, I trow,
 Are as tall and strong as they.
There are unmarked graves in the lonely South,
 There are spectres that walk at will,—
But the flag that you saved at the cannon's mouth
 Is the flag that is over you still.

The flag thro' the shot and the shell that you bore,
  And wrapped in your blouses blue,
The flag that your swore to defend evermore,
  Is the flag of the Union too.

THE OLD FLAG.

BRONZED and bearded the veterans stood; their
    ranks were sparse and slim;
And the Colonel standing before them felt his eyes
    grow strangely dim;
He thought of the muster, he thought of the march,
    he thought of a darker day,
And he thinks he hears through the hush of years
    the sharp artillery play;
And he sees the flashing of burnished steel, and the
    hurrying cannoneer;
And he hears, while his heart leaps up again, the
    long-roll sounding clear,
And the *rub, rub, rub-a-dub dub,* falls sharp on his
    listening ear.

The Colonel stood with head bowed down, and his
    breast heaved hard and fast,
As he thought of the parting and thought of the
    pain and thought of the dangers past,

Of Bob, and Willie, and John, and Jim,—of the
    brave lads sent to death
With the kisses pressed by a mother's lips kept warm
    to their dying breath ;
He thought of the pride of his men so true, as they
    swept on the enemy's lines,
He thought of their valor, as, crouched and cold,
    they fought in the pitiless pines,
Mid the *rub, rub, rub-a-dub dub,* and the flashing of
    hidden mines.

The Colonel's voice is so loud and strong he could
    rally a whole brigade,
With his charge in the face of the enemy's guns, in
    the din of the cannonade ;
But now, as he speaks, for the smothered tears you
    can scarcely his story learn,
He speaks so slow and he speaks so low to the hearts
    that within us burn,—
He speaks so slow and he speaks so low, for he tells
    of a sore defeat,
With the color-guard felled like a dog to the earth
    and the colors beneath his feet,
While the *rub-a-dub dub, dub, rub-a-dub dub,* is beat-
    ing a slow retreat.

As brave as a lion our color-guard stood ; but they
    charged us three to one,
And our lines fell back in ruin and wrack from the
    havoc of grape and gun —
Fell back with a comrade's cry in their ears and a
    comrade's pain in their heart,
And the ghastly stare of the shattered slain forever
    of life a part,—
With the rifled dead, and the riddled blue, and the
    flag of their dear desire,
To serve as the trophies of jeer and jest around an
    enemy's fire,
And the *rub-a-dub dub, dub, rub-a-dub dub*, a dirge
    for their funeral pyre.

The Colonel said : " It is sad, my men, that now
    that the war is done,
And we come to talk of the troubles past, and the
    dawn of a gladder sun,
That still in the van of our broken ranks the old
    flag may not go,—
It lies, with the pride of our regiment, at the feet
    of a mocking foe ;
We may boast our triumphs, and count our scars,
    and dream of a great reward,

But the flag that has led us through thick and thin
    is down with the color-guard,
Where no *rub-a-dub dub, dub, rub-a-dub dub*, may
    sweep o'er the peaceful sward."

Then over the bronzed and bearded men a tremor
    of gladness swept,
As one by one they drew from their breasts a
    trophy that each had kept;
And one, with a trembling in his voice, that was
    more of joy than tears,
Stood up to speak for the battle-scarred ranks of
    the veteran volunteers,—
And they marked him well as a valiant man in the
    march or the fiercest fight,
Who never had swerved when the call was close, to
    the left, or yet to the right,
While the *rub, rub, rub-a-dub dub*, was calling for
    men of might.

And he said, " My Colonel, 'twas I stood by when
    our color-guard fell that day,
And under the stress of unequal strength our regi-
    ment melted away,

2

And I tore, ere I went, the tattered rags that clung
    to the staff of oak,
That has led us to victory time on time through
    the cloud and the fire and the smoke,
And I folded them close to my heart, just here; for
    I could not then forget
If the boys could but look on their colors snatched
    from the hell of that parapet,
That the *rub-a-dub dub, dub, rub-a-dub dub*, would
    lead them to victory yet."

They gathered around their Colonel so dear; and
    each had a tattered shred
Of the flag that had cheered on the living, that had
    rallied their comrades dead;
And they stitched with the fragments of glory the
    thoughts of a holier day—
Of the gallant and true whose red rich blood still
    mottled it where it lay;
And up from a staff, new-carven, they raised the
    sacred thing,
And wildly and yet more wildly the cheers of the
    veterans ring,
While *rub-a-dub dub, dub, rub-a-dub dub*, exultant
    the tidings wing.

O flag of our fathers ! O flag of our sons ! O flag
    of a world's desire !

Through the night and the light, through the fright
    and the fight, through the smoke and the cloud
    and the fire,

There are arms to defend, there are hearts to be-
    friend, there are souls to bear up from the pall,

While thy cluster of stars broodeth over the wars,
    that justice and mercy befall !

There are breasts that will clasp it when tattered
    and torn, there are prayers to brood like a dove,

There are fingers to fashion it fold unto fold, and
    hands that will wave it above,

While the *rub-a-dub dub, dub, rub-a-dub dub*, is beat-
    ing the marches of Love !

ULRIC DAHLGREN.

A FLASH of light across the night,
  An eager face, an eye afire !
O lad so true, you may yet rue
  The courage of your deep desire !

" Nay, tempt me not; the way is plain—
  'Tis but the coward checks his rein;
    For there they lie
    And there they cry
For whose dear sake 'twere joy to die ! "

He bends unto his saddle bow,
  The steeds they follow two and two ;
Their flanks are wet with foam and sweat,
  Their riders' locks are damp with dew.

" O comrades, haste ! the way is long,
  The dirge it drowns the battle song ;
    The hunger preys,
    The famine slays,
An awful horror veils our ways ! "

Beneath the pall of prison wall
   The rush of hoofs they seem to hear ;
From loathsome guise they lift their eyes,
   And beat their bars and bend their ear.

" Ah, God be thanked! our friends are nigh ;
He wills it not that thus we die ;
     O fiends accurst
     Of Want and Thirst,
Our comrades gather, — do your worst ! "

A sharp affright runs through the night,
   An ambush stirred, a column reined ;
The hurrying steed has checked his speed,
   His smoking flanks are crimson stained.

O noble son of noble sire,
Thine ears are deaf to our desire !
     O knightly grace
     Of valiant race,
Thy grave is honor's trysting-place !

O life so pure ! O faith so sure !
   O heart so brave, and true, and strong !
With tips of flame is writ your name,
   In annaled deed and storied song !

It flares across the solemn night,
It glitters in the radiant light ;
A jewel set,
Unnumbered yet,
In our Republic's coronet !

FOREVER AND FOREVER.

WHEN men forsook their shops and homes, and
    stood with troubled faces
From morn till night, from night till morn, in dusty
    market spaces ;
When women watched beside their babes in anguish
    half resisted,
Until the husky message came : *" God keep you,
    I've enlisted ! "*
When all day long the drums were rolled in hateful
    exultation,
And fife and bugle stung with pain the pulses of the
    Nation ;
When woman's hand formed every star that flashed
    on field of glory,
And woman's tears were stitched along each stripe
    in jeweled story,—

What said we then ? *" Go forth, brave hearts ! Go
    where the bullets rattle !
For us to plan, for us to pray, for you to toil and
    battle !*

Ours to uphold, yours to defend, the compact none
*   can sever ;*
And sacred be your name and fame, forever and
*   forever ! "*

When charge and trench gave up their dead, and
    loathsome Southern prison ;
When on the march the hidden shot took aim with
    swift precision ;
When every whitewashed ward put out the light of
    some lone dwelling,
And every lumbering ambulance some dying plaint
    was telling ;
When fathers took their papers up with sense of
    evil presage,
And mothers tore with stifling sobs the wrap of
    some swift message ;
When prone the people lay before their God with
    sins uncovered,
And with overshadowing awfulness the black-
    winged angel hovered,—

What said we then ? *" Stand firm, brave hearts !*
stand where the bullets, crashing,

*Cut down your comrades as the sheaves go down before
    the threshing !*
*A Nation pleads with lifted hands, ' Give up the
    Union, never ! '*
*And yours the glory that abides, forever and for-
    ever ! "*

When bronzed and scarred and tattered sore, the
    ranks of dusty blue
Came up from Appomattox with their banners rid-
    dled through,
An hundred for a thousand, and by tens where
    fifties went,
With their armless sleeves and crutches showing
    where the balls were spent ;
When they stacked their trusty rifles and their knap-
    sacks flung aside,
And made known their comrades' messages to loved
    ones ere they died,
When the Nation breathed more freely than for ten
    long years before,
Though crape hung, freshly knotted, upon many a
    muffled door,—

What said we then ? *"O tried and true who live to
    rise and rally,*
*O tried and true who sleep so well by storied stream
    and valley!*
*We bind this debt upon our hearts, which time cannot
    dissever,*
*To guard your name and shield your fame, forever
    and forever !"*

When fort and rifle-pit are brought unto a common
    level,
And where the soldier's blood ran red, the long
    wild-grasses revel ;
When year by year the ranks go down that thrilled
    to deeds of glory,
And year by year the ear grows cold to patriotic
    story ;
When men forget, in stocks and trade and fevered
    speculation,
That any smote and any saved the honor of the
    Nation ;
When policy would blot the names of hero and of
    battle,
And swear we never saw a foe or heard a musket
    rattle,—

What say we now? "*O comrade hearts that still
    are strongly bounding,*
*And comrade hearts that wake no more to catch the
    bugle's sounding;*
*As when you fought, as when you fell, your mem-
    ory gladdens ever;*
*Our faith is wedded to your fame, forever and for-
    ever!*"

No more the cartridge answers in the rifle true and
    trusty,
And the good sword lies neglected in its scabbard
    dim and rusty;
The blue and gray no longer are the colors of
    division,
And "Yank" and "Reb" are heard no more the
    nicknames of derision;
The malice of the combat is, thank God, no longer
    cherished,
The vengeance that relents not in the breasts of all
    has perished,
And an infinite compassion in each loyal heart is
    swelling
For the vanquished in the shadows of each deso-
    lated dwelling,—

Yet say we now, as in the days of our humilia-
tion,
As in the days when triumph crowned the armies
of the Nation :
*"The men who fought, the men who fell, the old flag
none can sever,*
*Shall all be shrined in loyal hearts, forever and for-
ever ! "*

O shadow-armies, bending where the roses shed
to-day
Their gentle fragrance typical of all our hearts
would say,
From the spires of the Atlantic to the Golden Gate
sublime
Where Thomas waits his old reserves who're serving
out their time !
O shadow-armies, bending where the drooping lilies
weep,
With the watchers broken-hearted who slumber not
nor sleep !
O shadow-armies, bending from the summits of the
stars,
Bearing up the flying pennons of the dear old
Stripes and Stars,—

Bear witness that we keep to-day the vows that we
    have spoken,

In our iliads, in our anthems, in our prayers weak
    and broken ;—

In our statues proudly rising, in the statutes none
    can sever,

From the records of a Union, sealed forever and
    forever !

MEMORIAL DAY AT ANDERSONVILLE, 1884.

O COMRADES, on each lonely grave we place one
    flower to-day,
More sweet than any that shall bloom upon the
    heart of May;
More flush in blue and crimson, with starry splendor
    crowned,
Because the thunders raged above, the darkness
    hemmed around ;
The flower that our fathers saw, an hundred years
    before,
A tiny tendril springing by the lonely cabin door ;
'Twas sown in fears, 'twas wet with tears, till, lo, it
    burst in view,
The symbol of a Nation's hopes — the Red, the
    White, the Blue.

Ah, not in anger, not in strife, we come with laden
    hands ;
The crimson retinues of War are off in other lands ;

We bring the blossoms we have nursed to shed
their honeyed breath
Where erst the reeling ranks of wrath unbarred the
gates of death ;
We lift the dear dead faces of our heroes to the
light,
We raise the pallid hands of theirs, we clasp and
hold them tight ;
We say : O brothers, rise and see the Peace you
helped to woo,
Whose snowy pinions hover o'er the Red, the
White, the Blue.

Not yours, O silent comrades, the ecstacy of strife,
The haughty exaltation that rounds the hero's life ;
Not yours the flash of sabers, the shouts of the
advance,
The gleam of thrusting bayonets that shiver as they
glance;
Not yours upon the parapet your banner to unfurl,
To die with victory on your lips, as back your feet
they hurl ;
The whisper of a kindling hope, while gaily over
you

The silken folds are dancing out — the Red, the
   White, the Blue.

Nay, to your homesick vision the mask of Death
   was up,
His icy breath was round you, his draught was in
   the cup ;
A terror walks at noonday ; the dreams that throng
   the night
But take the wings of morning and vanish ere the
   light.
But oh, our fallen heroes, one gleam of heaven
   shines
Upon the ghastly phalanxes, along the ragged lines,
And eyes grown dim with watching are lit with
   courage new,—
They've heard the tramp of comrades, with the
   Red, the White, the Blue.

O comrades of the prison, ye have not died in
   vain,
For lo, the march of harvests where War has trod
   the plain !
And lo, the breath of lilies and of rose beyond
   compare,

And the sound of children chanting where the
cannon rent the air !
We clasp our hands above you with tearful hearts
to-day,—
Your brothers who have worn the blue, your
brothers of the gray ;
Our hearts are one forever, whatever men may do,
And over all the glory of the Red, the White, the
Blue.

Ah, not in strife nor anger nor idle grief we come,
With thrill and throb of bugle, with clamor of the
drum ;
We've heard the wings of healing above the war's
surcease,
And lo, the Great Commander has set the watch-
word, " Peace ! "
Peace to the free-born millions who live to do and
dare,
Peace in each brave endeavor, in whatever lot they
share !
Above, the triune colors, so dear to me and you,
The splendid flower that Freedom guards — the
Red, the White, the Blue.

3

THOMAS AT CHICKAMAUGA.

It was that fierce contested field when Chickamauga lay
Beneath the wild tornado that swept her pride
 away ;
Her dimpling dales and circling hills dyed crimson
 with the flood
That had its sources in the springs that throb with
 human blood.
" *Go say to General Harker to reinforce his right!* "
Said Thomas to his *aide-de-camp*, when wildly went
 the fight ;
In front the battle thundered, it roared both right
 and left,
But like a rock "Pap" Thomas stood upon the
 crested cleft.

"*Where will I find you, General, when I return ?* "
 The aide
Leaned on his bridle-rein to wait the answer
 Thomas made ;

The old chief like a lion turned, his pale lips set
    and sere,
And shook his mane, and stamped his foot, and
    fiercely answered, "*Here!*"

The floodtide of fraternal strife rolled upward to his
    feet,
And like the breakers on the shore the thunderous
    clamors beat ;
The sad earth rocked and reeled with woe, the
    woodland shrieked in pain,
And hill and vale were groaning with the burden of
    the slain.

Who does not mind that sturdy form, that steady
    heart and hand,
That calm repose and gallant mien, that courage
    high and grand? —
O God, who givest nations men to meet their lofty
    needs,
Vouchsafe another Thomas when our country
    prostrate bleeds !

They fought with all the fortitude of earnest men
    and true—

The men who wore the rebel gray, the men who
wore the blue ;
And those, they fought most valiantly for petty
state and clan,
And these, for truer Union and the brotherhood of
man.

They come, those hurling legions, with banners
crimson splashed,
Against our stubborn columns their rushing ranks
are dashed,
Till 'neath the blistering iron hail the shy and
frightened deer
Go scurrying from their forest haunts to plunge in
wilder fear.

Beyond, our lines are broken; and now in frenzied
rout
The flower of the Cumberland has swiftly faced
about ;
And horse and foot and color-guard are reeling
rear and van,
And in the awful panic man forgets that he is
man.

Now Bragg, with pride exultant above our broken
    wings,
The might of all his army against "Pap" Thomas
    brings ;
They're massing to the right of him, they're mass-
    ing to the left,
Ah, God be with our hero, who holds the crested
    cleft !

Blow, blow, ye echoing bugles ! give answer,
    screaming shell !
Go, belch your murderous fury, ye batteries of hell !
Ring out, O impious musket ! spin on, O shat-
    tering shot,—
Our smoke encircled hero, he hears but heeds ye
    not !

Now steady, men ! now steady ! make one more
    valiant stand,
For gallant Steedman's coming, his forces well in
    hand !
Close up your shattered columns, take steady aim
    and true,
The chief who loves you as his life will live or die
    with you !

By solid columns, on they come ; by columns they
    are hurled,
As down the eddying rapids the storm-swept booms
    are whirled ;
And when the ammunition fails — O moment drear
    and dread—
The heroes load their blackened guns from
    rounds of soldiers dead.

God never set his signet on the hearts of braver
    men,
Or fixed the goal of victory on higher heights than
    then ;
With bayonets and muskets clubbed, they close the
    rush and roar ;
Their stepping-stones to glory are their comrades
    gone before.

O vanished majesty of days not all forgotten yet,
We consecrate unto thy praise one hour of deep
    regret ;
One hour to them whose days were years of glory
    that shall flood
The Nation's sombre night of tears, of carnage,and
    of blood !

O vanished majesty of days, when men were
    gauged by worth,
Set crowned and dowered in the way to judge the
    sons of earth ;
When all the little great fell down before the great
    unknown,
And priest put off the hampering gown and coward
    donned his own !

O vanished majesty of days that saw the sun
    shine on
The deeds that wake sublimer praise than Ghent
    or Marathon ;
When patriots in homespun rose — where one was
    called for, ten—
And heroes sprang full-armored from the humblest
    walks of men !

O vanished majesty of days ! Rise, type and mould
    to-day,
And teach our sons to follow on where duty leads
    the way ;
That whatsoever trial comes, defying doubt and
    fear,
They in the thickest fight shall stand and proudly
    answer " *Here !* "

THE GRAND ARMY OF THE REPUBLIC.

MESEEMED a vision filled the night, of strong men
   mustering,
And two by two in solemn pride they strode with
   sturdy swing;
I stood upon the battlements and saw them man
   the guns,
And fling the halyards to the breeze where mad
   mid-ocean runs;
To right of me, to left of me, they rallied, man and
   man,
Until, meseemed, the plains were groves, the groves
   like rivers ran;
I heard the scream of bugles and the throbbing of
   the drums,
As the murmur of the thunders that portend the
   storm that comes.
My pulses stung and trembled, my blood was all afire,
To see the sons go stalking forth, to battle, with
   their sire;

" *God keep my first-born darling,*" the mother knelt
  to pray,—
And so our great Grand Army was mustered in
  that day.

Up springs the stalwart Lincoln — God grant his
  spirit 's near !
And as he calls the roll of States, they rise and
  answer: " *Here !* "
Maine shouts to Minnesota, Vermont to Oregon:
" *Who hails the sword of Bunker Hill, rise up and
  put it on !* "
The flame has lit the forges, the engines pant and
  fret,
And lo! upon the hilltops the signal fires are set:
The shade of Ethan Allen is up and marching now,
And Henry fires the forum, and Putnam leaves the
  plow.
Who stems the tide of battle, he does it at his cost,
Who stays a hand where Freedom leads, he is
  forever lost;
The list of heroes lengthens, a splendor gilds the
  scroll,—
And so our great Grand Army made up its battle
  roll.

Oh, there was brave maneuver in sight of foe and
    friend,
And toss of plume and feather, and marching
    without end;
And there were banners waving, and there were
    songs and cheers,
And for the patriot praises, and for the coward
    jeers;
And here the splendid Infantry accoutered bright
    and blue,
And there the gleaming trappings of Cavalry in
    view;
And flash of scarlet gunners and riders in the line,
With gorgeous spreading epaulettes and sashes red
    as wine;
And lo, the long processions of maidens drawing
    nigh,
With kisses and with flowers, to say a last good-
    bye;
And lo, the wives a-lifting their babies to the sun,—
And so our great Grand Army beheld its work
    begun.

I turned me to the Southland, and War swept
    into view,

With Famine and with Fever a-riding one and two;
And there was clash and clamor and marshaling
    for the fray,
And in the shock of battle, they met, the Blue and
    Gray;
'Tis brother met with brother, 'tis match of man
    and man,
The jousts of peers and princes upon a mightier
    plan;
The red, red tide of battle is sweeping on its way,
With hope and heart and fortune, forever and a
    day.
But not in knightly crusade or quest of Holy
    Grail
Were purer hands uplifted, did holier vows pre-
    vail;
Nor e'en to good Sir Galahad were saintlier visions
    sent,
Than in our great Grand Army to dying eyes were
    lent.

Play up, O fife and bugle! play up, sonorous drum!
The legions of disunion, they tremble as ye come!
Play up the blue Potomac! play up along the
    James!

Where patriot cheers are swelling, where rebel
    laughter shames !
Play up the slopes of Lookout! play up both loud
    and fast,
For Farragut's at Mobile, and lashed unto the
    mast !
Play up for Appomattox, and let your tunes be
    gay,
For underneath the apple-tree the Blue has met
    the Gray !
Play up the flag of Freedom ! play up the Stripes
    and Stars !
Play down the rag of Treason ! play down the Stars
    and Bars !
Play up the " March through Georgia," night can
    not always last !
Play up our great Grand Army ! God speed it,
    first and last !

With faded coat and feather, the thin battalions
    come,
And here the drooping banner, and there the
    muffled drum ;
The gleam of splendid trappings may nevermore
    be told,

The scarlet and the crimson, the glitter and the
 gold.
Within the awful prisons the ragged ranks are
 mute,
With never a dirge lamenting and never a last
 salute ;
And many a brave battalion goes down forever-
 more,
Since War has supped with Fever while Famine
 kept the door.
And lo, beyond the prison, beyond the faded lines,
The sad and slow processions go sadly 'mong the
 pines :
The maidens and the mothers a-searching for the
 slain,
Who with our great Grand Army will never come
 again.

Unite your ranks, O comrades ! consolidate bri-
 gades !
Call in vidette and picket ! suspend your dashing
 raids !
Take home your captured cannon and mould them
 into stars,

To deck the breasts of veterans returning from the
    wars !
Swing out the tattered banners, though riddled
    through and through ;
With elbow touching elbow begin your Grand
    Review ;
Was ever seen such marching, say, comrades,
    'neath the sun,
As army meeting army you made at Washington ?
The hilltops are exultant ! the streets with joy are
    wild,
And the veteran's heart is thrilled with thoughts of
    home and wife and child ;
Cheers meeting cheers resounding make up a sea
    of sound,
That lauds our great Grand Army wherever fame
    is found !

Play up ! play up, ye bugles ! play up, both fife
    and drum !
But not from wars returning to-day our comrades
    come !
Maine calls to Minnesota, Vermont to Oregon :
" *Who hails the sword of Bunker Hill, rise up and
    journey on !* "

The picket-guards of Freedom are on the outward
line,

And on the heights of victory their banners we
define ;

They wage a grander warfare than any has been
told,

And prairie yields her treasure and mountain gives
her gold.

Play up, play up the music to which our comrades
fell,

The tunes that in a hundred fights they loved both
long and well !

Play up, where freemen gather ! wherever man
meets man,

'Tis there our great Grand Army is ever in the
van !

Play up, O fife and bugle ! play up, sonorous
drum !

Play up the hosts of Freedom rejoicing as they
come !

Play up the war-worn soldiers, wherever they may
stand !

Play up the old Potomac ; play up the Cumberland !

The veterans are coming, be still my heart and
    hear,
It is the glad hosanna, it is the Union cheer !
Heaven speed the fight they're making ! Heaven
    give to each his due,
Who bore the brunt of battle to keep the Union
    true !
Play up, while lo, before them we lay our brightest
    flowers,
While mirth and song and laughter beguile the
    golden hours !
From Maine to Minnesota, play up our comrades
    true,
Who in our great Grand Army have worn the
    Union blue.

Play up the march of Empire ! play up the march
    of Love !
The mighty West before us ! the Stars and Stripes
    above !
Play up the South returning ! play up the reveille ;
Play up for truer Union ! play up for States to be !
Play up the struggling nations whose eyes have
    hailed the morn

That glows above the cradle where Liberty was
   born !
Play up the toiling millions, whose race is but
   begun ;
Play up, play up for Lincoln ! Play up for Washington !
Play up the Union rally ! play up both loud and
   shrill :
One heart, one hope, one faith, one flag, shall be our
   slogan still !
Play up the " March through Georgia," your
   merriest music play !
Play up our great Grand Army forever and for
   aye !

THE McPHERSON STATUE.

[Unveiled at Clyde, O., July 22, 1881.]

O FRIENDS, why gather you here to-day in the flush
    of the golden weather,
With your arms reversed and your colors furled, and
    your heads bowed low together ?
There are cheers for the victor, and flowers for the
    bride, and songs for the happy-hearted,
And a prayer for the soul that is groping alone in
    the shadows that time has started ;
There's a kiss for the child, and a ring for the bride,
    and a rose for the happy lover,
There are smiles for the guest, and a rosy nest that
    the last-born babe may cover ;
There's a laugh for the feast, and a gift for the
    priest ; there are vows for the holy altar ;
But what has the valley of death for him in whose
    praises our voices falter ?

"O Jamie McPherson, Jamie McPherson!"   The
    cry is the cry of a mother ;

But the little lad goes, and the little lad comes no
    more beside sister or brother ;

The little lad goes, and the cherished chief comes
    a prince in his pride and his valor ;

And the hero-heart thrills as it fills with his fame,
    and the craven is ashen with pallor.

"*O Jamie McPherson, Jamie McPherson!*" The
    cry is the cry of a Nation,

For the prince in his pride lieth low in the trail and
    the trampling of sore tribulation.

The brave heart is dust and the bright sword is rust,
    and under the sod he is lying,

Whose heart was a babe's in the lovelight of peace,
    and a lion's when bullets were flying.

As over the grave of her first-born son the mother
    in infinite yearning

Remembers each kiss and each touch of the hand
    from the gloom of the shadows returning,

Recalls all the grace of the best-beloved face as she
    scatters the lilies and roses,

While a tear on each stem like a diadem the wealth
    of devotion discloses,—

So over the grave of her hero to-day the Nation in
    sorrow is bending,

The rose of regret and the roses of love with the
lilies of memory blending ;
The grace of the lily, the pride of the rose, that
sweet in the heart are a-blowing,
Where the soil is a prayer, and the dew is a tear, and
a-sorrow the hand that is sowing.

Before this mute image of soldierly pride, ye comrades who loved him, uncover !
No lordlier man than it symbols e'er rode with the
ranks of the knight or the lover ;
No statelier form wore the blue and the gold, and
the shimmer of stars on his shoulder,
With a steadier mien and a steadier heart and a step
that was truer and bolder.
No voice with a call that was clearer rang out where
the columns were forming,
No chief with an eye that was keener swept on
where the battle was storming—
Sped the charge of the lines, scaled the crest of the
pines, bore down to the carnage the faster,
Lay calmly to rest with face to the foe in the gloom
of a direr disaster.

Before this mute image of greatness, dear sons of
    the commonwealth, tarry !
For here were the virtues that nations extol, the
    graces that princes should carry ;
The courage to toil, and the life without soil, the
    filial faith, and the largess
Of spirit that follows where Fealty leads the fire of
    her furious charges ;
The hero to place and the hero to plan in the whirl
    of the maddening clamor,
Where the bravest turn pale and the boldest are
    dumb and the lips of the eloquent stammer.
Aye, tarry and study ! the models are few, and the
    men of his mould are fast falling ;
Bow down in the dust when ye list to their names,
    their mighty achievements recalling.

Dear land of our love, dear land of our hopes ! till
    the pride of the patriot perish,
The deeds they have wrought, and the fame they
    have won, in the heart of our hearts we will
    cherish.
The valleys we till and the mountains we scale that
    girdle the zone of the Nation

Are greater and grander because they ran red with
    the wine of their soul's consecration ;
And the hopes of the brave, and the loves of the
    true, and the aim of each earnest endeavor,
In the sun of their greatness shall ripen and yield in
    the cycles of memory ever :
In the purpose to dare and the courage to bear, in
    the glory of high aspiration,
In the clasp of a hand and the flight of a prayer, in
    the beauty of pure adoration.

O Jamie McPherson ! Jamie McPherson ! when men
    of thy model He giveth,
Eye looks unto eye, and heart calls unto heart,
    " *Though darkness be over, God liveth*,"
So the weak are made bold and the strong are held
    true, and a Voice stays the storm's awful
    power,
And the smiles of a Love that embraces the world
    fall down in a scintillant shower.
O Jamie McPherson ! Jamie McPherson ! As they
    mingle their praises who love thee,
Ohio, thy fond mother, blesses to-day the honors
    she gathers above thee :

Thou, flower and fruit of her motherhood's dream,
    brave son of her prophesied glory,
Immortal in name and undying in fame, and match-
    less in epic and story !

Let the marble and bronze tell the deeds of thy fame,
    and the lily and rose how we love thee,
While the grasses grow greener that over thee wave,
    and the breezes blow blither above thee ;
For the seasons may come, and the seasons may go,
    and the lilies and roses may cover,
But no statelier chief or no faithfuler friend shall
    ride down with the knight and the lover !
In the sleet and the snow, in the sun and the shine,
    in the days of a far generation,
Brave soldier ! keep guard, for thy type it is true,
    and thy shrine shareth love's adoration !
Keep watch and keep ward, while our sons shall
    keep guard o'er the banner that shadowed thee
    dying !
Keep watch and keep ward, while the Stripes and
    the Stars in the vanguard of nations is flying !

SIGHTLESS SCARS.

HE bears no wounds on each shapely limb,
  No scar on his sun-browned cheek,
The crash of the bullets have left to him
  No tremor of nerves grown weak ;
And yet he has lost, O God, how much,
  Of all that is dear to a man ! —
The strength to say " No " to the tempter's touch,
  And the will to arise from his ban.

" *He fought for the flag ?* " Aye, fought with his
    might,
  Though a boy with a beardless face,
And his breath was aflame as he sprang to the fight,
  Though his lips wore a nameless grace.
Who saw him are sure he would freely have given
  His life for his country's weal ;
He sprang to the breach when the line was riven,
  As if with his body to heal.

None ever beheld his back to the foe,
  None heard a complaint or a sigh;
He was glad he could march with the serried row,
  He was glad he could dare to die;
But the heat and the cold, and the hunger and
    thirst,
  They warred with the shot and shell,—
And the lad found a balm in the cup accursed
  For the woes of a wilder hell.

Friend, give him a hand; he has given for you
  The whole that a man can give
Who yet must toil and yet must do
  What little he may to live;
He laid his hopes of a lifetime down
  When he donned the sword that day,
And put off the student's cap and gown
  To follow the troops away.

You stood heaping gold in the market-place;
  He scaled to the peaks of war; —
Now pause as you look in his war-worn face,
  And say whose the honors are!

And give him a hand as he gropes alone—
  A hand that is warm and true—
As God who sits on His judgment throne
  Shall judge betwixt him and you.

FALL IN.

FALL in, fall in, old soldiers !
　The reveille is heard,
And bivouac and picket
　Are at the summons stirred ;
Fall in, that you may answer
　The roll-call sounding clear,
And when the Sergeant calls your name
　Prepare to answer "*Here !*"

Fall in, fall in, old soldiers,
　And rub your sleepy eyes ;
The mists of time are heavy
　Around you as you rise ;
The friendships on the musket sworn
　Grow rusty as its lock ;
Fall in once more, touch elbows,
　As in the battle's shock.

Fall in, fall in, old soldiers,
　By whatever name you bear,—

If you've made the march through Georgia,
　If at Richmond you were there ;
If on Lookout's lofty tablets
　You've writ your names in blood,
If you've stemmed the hosts at Franklin,
　Pouring onward like a flood.

Fall in, fall in, old soldiers,—
　You who recall the day
At Corinth on the battlefield—
　The dead around you lay,
When Rosecrans rode down the lines
　To Fuller's old brigade :
" *I take my hat off in the face*
　Of men like these," he said.

Fall in, fall in, old soldiers,—
　You who from Red House Bridge
Moved on to Chickamauga
　When Thomas held the ridge ;
Moved on with gallant Steedman
　That day he broke away
Like a lion from his covert
　When he heard the battle bray.

Fall in, fall in, old soldiers ;
  Perchance you followed well
At Kenesaw with Harker
  And caught him when he fell ;
Perchance you joined the wild mad cry
  That through the army ran :
" *McPherson and revenge !* " then smote
  The foemen rear and van.

Fall in, fall in, old soldiers ;
  A glory crowns you still,
For marches under Sherman,
  For raids with " Little Phil."
Though you swore by Grant or Thomas,
  Or by Custer early dead,
There are roses for each bosom,
  There are laurels for each head.

Fall in, fall in, old soldiers ;
  Each day the ranks grow small,
Each day a voice grows silent
  Heard at the last roll-call ;
A comrade's voice makes answer
  Where was heard a manly shout :

" *Disabled in the service,*
   And awaits his muster-out! "

Fall in, fall in, old soldiers ;
   A few more flying years,
And roses will be blooming
   Above your lowly biers ;
The roses and the ivy
   And the lonely myrtle climb
Above the sleeping millions
   Plumed and knighted in their time.

Fall in, fall in, old soldiers,
   And fight your battles o'er,
Until above the last low bier
   The wings of Freedom soar ,
Stand hand to hand and heart to heart,
   In Fame's eternal care,
Until the great Reunion
   Unites you over there.

THE NATION'S MEMORIAL.

THE lowing cattle leave their stalls, the lambs bleat
    in the wold ;
The poplars don their tasseled caps with tips of
    burnished gold ;
The children in the streets are glad, and speed the
    hoop and ball,
Ne'er dreaming that a fear or foe could ever on
    them fall.

The hum of busy wheels is heard, the click of loom
    and press ;
The clearing axe resounds along the opening wil-
    derness ;
The air is filled with screaming birds that go from
    gulf to lake ;
And Spring in all the Northern vales is calling :
    " Rise ! Awake ! "

The mother sits beside her son and marks his eager
    joy

In reading how from Ghent to Aix rode the brave
  Flemish boy ;
How one by one the Old Guard fell, pierced through
  at Waterloo,
With England's flaunting flag of truce full flutter-
  ing to their view.

She sees him take his father's sword he wore at
  Monterey,
When wounded in his good right arm, among the
  dead he lay ;
She notes the hot blood flush his cheek, the glitter
  in his eye,
And says, " Thank God, no duty calls my boy to
  bleed or die ! "

But hark ! from out the South there come such
  strange and sudden cries
That every lad flings down his bat and stands with
  frightened eyes ;
The mills are hushed ; the presses groan ; the ham-
  mers silent fall ;
And fear on all the anxious streets has settled like
  a pall.

To arms! to arms! to arms! it comes, as when
some muttering storm
Along the threatened vales sends first its sullen
slow alarm ;
To arms! to arms! to arms! it swells, as when the
thunders crash
Among the swaying tree-tops where the lurid lightnings flash.

"God keep my boy !" the mother says, and straps
his knapsack down,
And sets the drooping cap of blue upon his golden
crown ;
"God keep my boy !" and by his side she proudly
follows on,
Nor fails nor faints, till out of sight the volunteers
have gone.

Behold a mighty angel, sifting, sifting as he flies !
The Nation 'tis he sifteth ! and behold before him
rise
Heroic men and women, whose consecrated prayers
Bring down the heights of victory like links of
golden stairs.

5

March on! march on! the blazing towns are telling
 where they halt !
March on! march on! the heath their bed, their
 shelter heaven's vault !
March on! while yet one foe remains to lift an impious hand
And tear the flag of Freedom from one cabin in the
 land !

Now with the corps of pioneers, the troops a road
 to hew,
Now leading on the skirmish line, the enemy in
 view;
Now scaling up the mountain's peak the foot of
 man ne'er trod,
The soldiers of the Union wage the battles blest
 of God.

Whiz, whiz, the flying minie-balls like leaden rain
 sweep on ;
Crash, crash, the rattling musketry, and rank by
 rank is gone ;
Roar, roar, the cannon thunders, and the air is black
 as night ;
And upward with the billows float our heroes souls
 from sight.

"Come hither now, my Captain, and tell, and tell
me true,
Where is my boy, my brave, good boy, who marched
away with you ?
O speak, that I may find him, that upon his mother's
breast
He may in all his agony one little moment rest.

"I've brought him, see, some simple things he
always liked at home,
Some grapes from our own garden — he will smile
to see me come !
Lead on—the moments hasten, and I must be with
my boy !
Dead, dead, your face makes answer ! Christ be
pitiful !" . . . . Deploy

Ye soldiers, for the battle ! Marshal, march in all
your pride,
But, behold, a spirit walketh close by every soldier's
side ;
And above the pæans rising float the murmurs of
the dirge,
As the moaning of the ocean drowns the clamor of
the surge.

Oh, ye cannot by your marching give the mother
   back her son,
Give the maiden back her lover, give the wife her
   dearest one ;
Give the little children calling, when the evening
   draws apace,
" Papa, papa !   Come home, papa ! " one more
   glimpse of his dead face.

But ye may rebuild the altars the despoiler has
   defiled,
And ye may restrain the sacrifice to idol fierce and
   wild ;
And, as from Sinai's holy height, announce the new
   command :
" Victoria, Victoria ! Freedom shall rule the land ! "

Now banners wave, and bugles blow, and woods
   with song be glad !
The house-tops throng with people, and the streets
   with joy run mad !
The cheers of Boston proudly up to Bunker Hill
   arise,
And westward roll and mingle as the Golden Gate
   replies !

Bring out the gray-haired veterans of Harrison and
    Clay,
And let them swing their hats once more on this
    eventful day !
Bring out the Buena Vista guards who stood by
    Taylor well,
And let them with their gallant cheers the shouts of
    triumph swell !

Bring out the little children, clad in fleecy robes of
    white,
To shout, with all their happy souls, their wild and
    glad delight !
And don't forget a place for those whose mute lips
    make no sign, —
Joy's sable guests of sorrow, moving slowly into
    line !

Time may fill all the furrows the cannon-balls have
    plowed ;
May set the robins singing where the bullets whistled
    loud ;
Time may the passion-flower twine o'er rude and
    ragged grave,
The poppy's flaunting pennons from the prison bur-
    rows wave ;

Time may set sirens singing where the good old ship
  sails true,—
But their voices wake no echo in the bosoms of the
  crew ;
Our hearts but beat the truer for the terrors we
  have past,
And the prophecies of ages live a verity at last.

Bend soft, O skies, above the graves our fallen
  heroes fill,
In far Potomac marshes, on the heights of Georgia
  hill,
Where the blue Virginia mountains in their lonely
  grandeur frown,
Where the tide of Chickamauga flows by fort-
  invested town !

Blow soft, O winds, around them with your freighted
  sweets and balm,
And the rhythm of your numbers flowing into song
  and psalm !
Say the Nation's heart is keeping, in its silent deeps
  aglow,
All the sacred recollections treasured in the long
  ago !

Smile soft, O flowers, bending low, like friends with
    saddened eyes,
Moist with the dear remembrances of saintly sac-
    rifice !
Rise, gracious lily ! Multiply, O rose, in regal
    pride !
Fit emblems of the loyal ones who lived, and loved,
    and died !

And thou, O flag of Freedom, fan their slumbers
    where they lie !
At morning toss and flutter, and at midnight float
    and fly !
Keep guard o'er all thy children as upon the walls
    they stood,
Baptising for futurity thy folds in crimson blood !

Float on above the living ; float on above the dead !
While a hope awaits fruition, while a prayer remains
    unsaid !
This motto on thy bosom bear to earth's remotest
    parts :
God keep the Union ! Give to all our people loyal
    hearts !

SONS OF VETERANS.

MUSTER the brave boys in !
Not for the clash of arms,
Not for the fierce alarms,
Not for the sword and the flame !
In the might of a Nation's name,
    Muster them in !

Muster the brave boys in !
Not for the reddening strife,
Not for "a life for a life,"
For the flight of furious steeds !
In the calm of a Nation's needs,
    Muster them in !

Muster the brave boys in !
Not for the gay parade,
Not for the reckless raid,
For the battles that rend the land !
In the love of a Nation's hand,
    Muster them in!

Muster the brave boys in !
Not for the smiting scourge,
Not for the awful dirge,—
For the graces that peace shall shed
Over a Nation's head,
        Muster them in !

Muster the brave boys in .
To stay the steps that are slow,
To lift the hearts that are low,
To stand as a guard of might
In the Nation's light, or night,
        Muster them in !

Muster the brave boys in !
That the vows may be passed along
That their fathers have kept and are strong,
In the hope of a happier day
In the Nation's heart for aye,—
        Muster them in !

DEAD ON THE BORDER.

Your soldier boy is gone ?
How fell he, comrade ? In the van
Where Death struck swift from man to man?
Oh, aye, I know he fell
Where the red raiders yell ;
    Our soldier boy is gone !

Your soldier boy is gone !
It was but yesterday he went
A lad with your old regiment,
Over the West Virginia hills,
Stout-hearted to the bugle trills !
    Our brave old boy is gone !

Your soldier boy has gone !
But yesterday, I said, and yet
A dozen harvest moons have set
Since on his shoulders shone the bars !
A valiant soul in valiant wars,
    Our brave good boy has gone.

Your soldier boy is gone !
O pallid face ! O cold, still heart !
O sweet veiled eyes whence no smiles start !
O stricken sword-arm ! Hear our prayer,
And answer if ye loved him, where
    Our soldier boy is gone ?

Your soldier boy is gone !
And what is left but sobs and tears,
But aching hearts and broken years?
Ah, God, have pity ! in thine eye
We are but babes that moan and cry !
    Our soldier boy is gone !

Your soldier boy is gone !
And nothing left but sobs and tears ?
Aye, memories of golden years,—
Fame, honor, manhood's royal meed
Of generous aim and glorious deed !
    Our soldier is not gone !

Your soldier boy is gone !
Aye, risen to heights sublimer far

Than any known to mortal are !
For, lo ! that life is deemed most blest
That serves its God and country best !
Our soldier is not gone !

HAIL TO THE FLAG.

RUMBLING, and rolling, and rocking, the battle swept
   up from the valley,
Laid its red hand on the harvest, its torch at the
   heart of the hearthstone ;
Laid its hot breath on the village, that shivered and
   shrank at its coming ;
Snapped like a forest of firs beneath the sharp
   strokes of the tempest.

Up from the hush of the hamlet came the low cries
   of the women,
Down from the whirl of the city, the wail of the
   fatherless children,
Mingling and making their moan in the lap of a
   desolate sorrow,—
The dirge and the funeral moan of a widowed and
   comfortless sorrow.

Day is as night, and the night is a sweeping and
   swift desolation,

The hurricane chained to its breast, and the curse
of the scourge in its footsteps ;
Heaping its dead in the trenches, with glitter of
steel, and the bayonet
Red like the Golgotha spear dipped in the blood of
the innocent.

Ever the long-roll is heard, the marching of men to
the slaughter,
The scream of the bugles like eagles that flap their
broad wings to the thunder ;
Mingling their din with the shriek of the shell and
the crash of the cannon,
And the shock of the lines as they kneel in solid
platoons to the volley.

" *Stand to your guns !* "   And there came the rush
and the crush of the whirlwind ;
Headless and trunkless they fell, the royal old oaks
of the forest,—
The men with the sinews of strength and the pride
of the oak-knotted forest,
Lay with their lips to the dust, and as dust the rent
reins of their valor.

Lay with their lips to the sod and their hearts to the
ribbed rocks as pulseless,
And the sobs of the ridges gave back the cries of
their soul in the conflict ;
The cry of the mighty struck dumb with their eyes
on the goal of the victor,
The waving of palms and the plumes, and the welcome acclaim to the victor.

Brothers they knelt in the ranks, with faces hard-
set for the battle,
And eyes that were eyes that beheld the march of
the gods in the war-dust,
The shimmer of shields and the plumes and the
stride of the gods in the war-dust ;
And the yawning wide earth at their feet with the
rumble of hell in its bosom.

Shoulder to shoulder they knelt in the glow and the
glare of the carnage,—
The red reeling whirl and the dance of the harpies
that gloat on the carnage ;
Stifled their souls in the heat and the thick blinding
smoke of the carnage,
The black-draught absinthe of hate drunk deep in
the wrath of the carnage.

Sighted their guns in the flash of the bursting of
    shell and the glamour
Of mad conflagration pent up in the mountain-
    locked depths of the forest ;
Sighted their guns as they lay with their hearts to
    the hearts of their comrades,
The long *abatis* of the dead thrown up at the feet
    of the living.

God ! how that terrible struggle is branded and
    burnt in my being,
Seared to my soul in the furnace of fiery and fierce
    tribulation !
Waking or sleeping, they rise and look in my eyes
    and confront me,
Look in my eyes with the eyes of the slain in the
    smoke of the battle.

Twain in the ranks they were mine, my foster sons
    born for the battle,
Stalwart of limb and of courage drawn from a long
    generation ;
A royal long lineage of men that fought on the
    moor and the mountain,
And planted the ensigns of Freedom high on the
    bulwarks of nations.

"Captain," he said, as he came, with one on each
    arm to the muster,
"Captain, we've talked it all over—I, and the boys,
    and their mother ;
And little we deem it of worth that we shrink when
    the need is supremest ;
Take them, and God help you, Captain, to make
    them half worthy their country."

Side by side in the ranks, in the camp, in the march,
    in the battle,
Side by side, my brave boys,—never a sigh nor a
    murmur ;
Deeming it honor to share the siege and the thirst
    and the hunger,
Deeming it honor, while forward beckoned the flag
    of the Union.

Death to the right and the left, ghostly and ghastly
    and gory,
Death in the sod at their feet, making its bitter com-
    plaining,
Death in the voice of the tempest, death in the gasp
    of a prayer,

6

Death — it is death but to speak, in the flight of a
thought it is hidden.

Keen as the lightning's breath the bullet has sped
on its mission ;
Forward the ranks are swept down, forward they
spring to the breaches ;
And ever the crash and the crush of the tempest of
fire, and the horror,
And ever the stretcher gives back the dust to the
earth that has given.

Side by side, my brave boys, my foster sons bred
for the battle,
Side by side in the smoke and the fire and the fierce
tribulation ;
Side by side with the seal of the angel of peace on
their bosom,
Under the rudely-turned sod waiting the dawn of
fruition.

Waiting the dawn of a day sweet as the birth of a
summer,
When like a bow in the clouds Union should span
the Republic ;

Flinging its halo of suns over the frosts of the
Northland,
Flinging its halo of stars over the dews of the
Southland.

Show me the men in the ranks, I will show you the
might of the Nation !
Crown them with laurels and love the battle-scarred
sons of our peril !
Sacred the hills where they lie, the plains that
received their baptismal,
Bright as the pathway of souls threading the arch-
way of heaven.

Would they might rise from the ranks, cordon the
hills, and confront us,
Lay their dead hands in our hands, awed in the
silver-tongued silence,
Under the pinions of peace, under the whispers of
promise,
Calmly with eye unto eye sharing the sweet bene-
diction.

What would they say, could they rise, look in our
eyes and salute us ?—

"*Men of the North and the South, nurtured in Liberty's cradle,*
Call it not vain that we fell bearing the ensigns of Union
High on the summits of fame, far on the outposts of Freedom.

"*Men of the North and the South, mighty in pride and in valor,*
Fair are the banners of Peace, brave is the service she offers ;
Broad are her fleets, and her sails lead to wide havens of conquest,
Proud are the forts that she storms, guarding the mints of the mountains.

"*Men of the North and the South, bitter the fountains of faction,*
Eschol has grapes that are sweet, valleys of milk and of honey ;
Turn from your idols, and forth, mount to the hills and possess them,
Fashion your temples of Peace, tribe unto tribe adding tribute

"Liberty calls from her heights : 'Give me brave men
for my service,
Men who can wrestle with wrong, armed with the
armor of honor;
Men who can stand with bared brows under the splen-
dors of heaven,
When the swift lightnings of wrath flash where the
storm-cloud is riven.' "

Lead us, O Liberty, lead, under the zenith of Hope,
Under the banners of Peace, tossing their fluttering
folds ;
   Under the shade and the sun,
   Blending their colors in one ;
   Red, White, and Blue,
   Blue, White, and Red,
Under the banners that float over our garlanded
dead.

Lead us, O Liberty, lead, forth to a holier day,
Glad with the cymbals of joy, great with the glory
to be ;
   Forth in the pride of our might,
   Forth in the might of the right ;

Red, White, and Blue,
Blue, White, and Red,
Under whose folds we have fought, under whose
stars we have bled.

Lead us, O Liberty, lead ! Happy who follow
anear,
Not as the conscripted go, not as the slave to his
chain,—
Strong in the sonship of love,
Strong in the grace from above ;
Red, White, and Blue,
Blue, White, and Red,
Emblem of happier hope, brothers to brotherhood
wed.

Lead us, O Liberty, lead, ready and steady we
come,
Elbow to elbow we march, timing our steps to the
call ;
Up from the ban and the blight,
Up to the summits of light ;
Red, White, and Blue,
Blue, White, and Red,
Conflict and carnage behind, glory and grandeur
ahead.

Lead us, O Liberty, lead, every star in its place,
Every fold of the dear old flag burning and bla-
zoned with love ;
> Below is the chastening rod,
> Above is the glory of God ;
> Blue, White, and Red,
> Red, White, and Blue,
Flag of our fathers, thrice hail ! Hail to the Red,
White, and Blue !

FOR HIS DEAR SAKE.

I HAVE gathered the dewy roses,
  The lily and columbine,
The ivy, and iris, and myrtle,
  And pale sweet jessamine ;
And out where some brave heart is lying
  In an unmarked lonely place,
For his dear, dear sake, I will strew them,
  Who slumbers at Rocky Face.

I woke when the odorous morning
  Came royally from the gloom,
And I wept as my gay companions
  Went culling from bloom to bloom ;
Ah, little they know of the sighing,
  And little of all the tears
That stifle the heart that is asking
  The loves of its happy years !

And I thought of the last fond message
  He sent in his hopeful way :

" But one little week, and I'm coming,
　　My Queen of the joyous May."
Now out in the wilds he is sleeping,
　　The where I may never see.
O May of the Mays ! — the gladdest
　　And saddest of all to me !

I know not where they have laid him,
　　My gallant, my brave, my own,—
Out, out where the wild fern is growing,
　　And the pines through the long years moan ;
And erst when the dead they have honored
　　With flowers and praiseful song,
I have lain in my darkened chamber
　　And murmured the whole day long.

But now I have gathered the flowers ;
　　And out where the lonely dove
Is making lament I will strew them
　　O'er some other woman's love ;
And may be in days that are coming,
　　With sorrow her sweet eyes dim,
Some other sad one will be strewing
　　May's beauteous blossoms o'er him.

THE DRUMMER BOY OF MISSION RIDGE.

[*Incident in the life of* JOHN S. KOUNTZ, *Commander-in-Chief*, *G.A.R.*]

DID ever you hear of the Drummer Boy of Mission
Ridge, who lay
With his face to the foe, 'neath the enemy's guns, in
the charge of that terrible day?
They were firing above him and firing below, and
the tempest of shot and shell
Was raging like death as he moaned in his pain, by
the breastworks where he fell.

We had burnished our muskets and filled our can-
teens, as we waited for orders that morn,—
Who knows when the soldier is dying of thirst where
the wounded are wailing forlorn? —
When forth from the squad that was ordered back
from the flash of that furious fire
Our Drummer Boy came, and his face was aflame
with the light of a noble desire.

"Go back with your corps !" our Colonel had said,
    but he waited the moment when
He might follow the ranks and shoulder a gun with
    the best of us bearded men ;
And so when the signals from old Fort Wood set an
    army of veterans wild,
He flung down his drum which spun down the hill
    like the ball of a wayward child.

And so he fell in with the foremost ranks of brave
    old Company G,
As we charged by the flank, with our colors ahead,
    and our columns closed up like a V,
In the long swinging lines of that splendid advance,
    when the flags of our corps floated out
Like the ribbons that dance in the jubilant lines of
    the march of a gala day rout.

He charged with the ranks, though he carried no
    gun, for the Colonel had said him nay,
And he breasted the blast of the bristling guns and
    the shock of the sickening fray ;
And when by his side they were falling like hail, he
    sprang to a comrade slain,
And shouldered his musket and bore it as true as
    the hand that was dead to pain.

'Twas dearly we loved him, our Drummer Boy, with
    a fire in his bright black eye,
That flashed forth a spirit too great for his form,—
    he only was just so high,
As tall perhaps as your little lad who scarcely
    reaches your shoulder,
Though his heart was the heart of a veteran then, a
    trifle, it may be, the bolder.

He pressed to the front, our lad so leal, and the
    works were almost won ;
A moment more, and our flags had swung o'er the
    muzzle of murderous gun ;
But a raking fire swept the van, and he fell 'mid the
    wounded and the slain,
With his wee wan face turned up to Him who feeleth
    His children's pain.

Again and again our lines fell back, and again with
    shivering shocks
They flung themselves on the Rebel works as the
    fleets on the jagged rocks ;
To be crushed and broken and scattered amain, as
    the wrecks of the surging storm,
Where none may rue and none may reck of aught
    that has human form.

So under the Ridge we were flying for the order to
    charge again,
And we counted our comrades missing and we
    counted our comrades slain ;
And one said, " Johnnie, our Drummer Boy, is
    grievously shot, and lies
Just under the enemy's breastworks ; if left on the
    field he dies."

Then all the blood that was in me surged up to my
    aching brow,
And my heart leaped up like a ball in my throat, I
    can feel it even now,
And I swore I would bring that boy from the field
    if God would spare my breath,
If all the guns on Mission Ridge should thunder the
    threat of death.

I crept and crept up the ghastly Ridge, by the
    wounded and the dead,
With the moans of my comrades right and left,
    behind me and yet ahead,
Till I came to the form of our Drummer Boy, in
    his blouse of dusty blue,
With his face to the foe, 'neath the enemy's guns,
    where the blast of the battle blew,

And his gaze as he met my own, God wot, would
    have melted a heart of stone,
As he tried like a wounded bird to rise, and placed
    his hand in my own ;
So wan and faint, with his ruby red blood drank
    deep by the pitiless sward,
While his breast with its fleeting, fluttering breath
    throbbed painfully slow and hard.

And he said in a voice half smothered, though its
    whispering thrills me yet,
"I think in a moment more that I would have stood
    on that parapet,
For my feet have trodden life's rugged ways, and I
    have been used to climb
Where some of the boys have slipped I know, but I
    never missed a time.

"But now I nevermore will climb; and, comrade,
    when you see
The men go up those breastworks there, just stoop
    and waken me ;
For though I cannot make the charge and join the
    cheers that rise,
I may forget my pain to see the old flag kiss the
    skies."

Well, it was hard to treat him so, his poor limb
    shattered sore,
But I raised him to my shoulder and to the Surgeon
    bore,
And the boys who saw us coming each gave a shout
    of joy,
Though some in curses clothed their prayers, for
    him, our Drummer Boy.

When sped the news that " Fighting Joe " had saved
    the Union right
With his legions fresh from Lookout, and that
    Thomas massed his might
And forced the Rebel center, and our cheering ran
    like wild,
And Sherman's heart was happy as the heart of a
    little child,—

When Grant from his lofty outlook saw our flags by
    the hundred fly
Along the slopes of Mission Ridge, where'er he cast
    his eye,
And our Drummer Boy heard the news and knew
    the mighty battle done,
The valiant contest ended, and the glorious victory
    won,—

Then he smiled in all his agony beneath the Surgeon's steel,
And joyed that his the blood to flow his country's
woes to heal ;
And his bright, black eyes so yearning, grew
strangely glad and wide ;
I think that in that hour of joy he gladly would
have died.

Ah, ne'er again our ranks were cheered by our little
Drummer's drum,
When *rub, rub, rub-a-dub dub*, we knew that our
hour had come ;
Beat brisk at morn, beat sharp at eve, rolled long
when it called to arms,
With *rub, rub, rub-a-dub dub*, 'mid the clamor of
rude alarms !

Ah, ne'er again our black-eyed boy looked up in the
veteran's face,
To waken thoughts of his children safe in mother
love's embrace !
O ne'er again with tripping feet he ran with the
other boys,—
His budding hopes were cast away as they were idle
toys.

But ever in our hearts he dwells, with a grace that
    never is old,
For him the heart to duty wed can nevermore grow
    cold !
His heart the hero's heart we name, the loyal, true,
    and brave,
The heart of the soldier hoar and gray, of the lad
    in his Southern grave !

And when they tell of their heroes, and the laurels
    they have won,
Of the scars they are doomed to carry, of the deeds
    that they have done,—
Of the horror to be biding among the ghastly
    dead,
The gory sod beneath them, the bursting shell o'er-
    head,—

My heart goes back to Mission Ridge and the
    Drummer boy who lay
With his face to the foe 'neath the enemy's guns in
    the charge of that terrible day ;
And I say that the land that bears such sons is
    crowned and dowered with all

The dear God giveth nations to stay them lest they
    fall

O glory of Mission Ridge! stream on, like the
    roseate light of morn,
On the sons that now are living, on the sons that
    are yet unborn !
And cheers for our comrades living, and tears as
    they pass away,—
And three times three for the Drummer Boy who
    fought at the front that day !

THE SOLDIER'S RING.

"O SIR, the ring, the ring!
The ring I gave you on that field of death !
I lay half gasping for the sluggish breath
That came and went and stayed so long that I
　　Thought I should die !
　　O sir, the ring, the ring !"

The woman fronts me now,
Standing before me with her great grave eyes
Wherein some burnt-out sorrow smouldering lies ;
Her lips close pressed to force the thrusting pain
　　To rest again ;
　　Athwart her lifted brow

The print of scoffings borne,
With thorn-crown forcing deadly drops ; her cheek
A storied page whereon the letters speak
Of tears that burn, and lips that yearn, and life
　　Seared in the strife
　　Where love, alas, lies lorn.

"O sir, the ring, the ring!"
Her trembling touch I feel, and lift my hand,
And take therefrom the gleaming beaten band,
And read thereon the letters, "C. E. D."
    And seemeth me
    The brooding years out-wing

    Unto Antietam's field ;
I tread among the dead ; I hear the groans
Of wounded men ; I hear the sighs and moans
Of homesick hearts; the plea of famished lips
    E'en for a drop that drips
    From founts unsealed ;

    And as we grope our way
With succor for sore hearts, we come to where
Among our fallen comrades, two are there
With heart so close to heart we marvel much
    If one fell touch
    Of sorrow did not slay ;

    Full-bearded, one, and brown,
With stalwart limbs and chest upheaved and strong,
We stoop to wake him.   Ah, his sleep is long,

That long, long sleep that knows
       Nor friends nor foes:
  We put his number down.

    But this pale lad who turns
A pleading face to meet the pitying eye,—
Ah, little lad, he surely shall not die!
Oh, cheer thee now, thou yet shall see the skies
       Where love-light lies,
  The hearth where home-light burns!

    I kneel and lift his hand—
Poor hand that gives no warm response to mine,—
Poor shattered hand so maiden-fair and fine!
And then the fainting plea: " Please take the ring,
       And wear it till I bring
  Words you may understand!"

    So with the vision gone,
And then, "O woman, what was he to thee?
A brother may be, or a lover?   See,
The ring I've worn these years, and in his name
       Whose heart aflame
  For country led him on!"

" Nay, brother he was not,
Nor lover, to whose thirsting lips you gave
From that canteen you brought to soothe and save!
'Twas I, a woman, whom you blessed that day !
    'Twas my love lay
  Close by as one forgot.

" Our wedding-day was set,
And happy plans were laid for happy days,
And love went merry in a hundred ways ;
When, one strange morning,—I can never tell
    How it befell,
  Grief stuns me even yet,—

" He came with hurrying pace,
And flushing cheek, and eye a-gleam with pride,
And said, ' My darling, my long-promised bride,
Our country now has need of me, I know,
    And so I go!'
  We stood there face to face,

" And yet I did not speak,
Nor utter a complaint, nor breathe a sigh.
Then came the words, ' God bless you, and ' Good-
    bye'!

He who was father, mother, friend in one,
      Was gone, and there was none—
   Alas for lives so bleak—

   " To comfort or to keep.
As one both blind and dumb, I stood apace ;
Meseemed that some vast hand had struck my face,
And seized me swiftly in its cruel grasp ;
      And from its clasp
   A thousand fears did leap

   " And rend me with fierce jaws ;
And then the sullen stupor come to lay
Its deathly clutch upon me day by day ;
And after that, O joy ! the dawn of hope
      My swooning sense to ope
   To Love's most blessed laws.

   " To cut my long brown hair,
And idly lounge where idle men were met
To prate of battles won and lost ; to let
The mustering sergeant take my age and name
      And whence I came ;
   To lift my hand and swear ;

"To doff my borrowed guise,
And don the envied suit of loyal blue;
The while they said: 'Poor boy! if he but knew
What woes there wait for those who go to war,
  Then were he far
  To venture in such wise,'—

"Thus sped the spell;
And hope and I are once more face to face,
Though death and danger follow on apace!
The drums play up, the banners dance ahead;
  Farewell to dread;
  Or life, or death, 'tis well!

"Aye, and I held my own,
And kept my pace beside the best of them,
And bore fatigues as did the rest of them;
Nor shrank when 'Forward' was the call to go
  Face to face with the foe
  Where the long lines were thrown.

"When we led the advance
At Antietam there, with the old Ninth Corps,
I marched by his side well up to the fore;

Over the ford at the old stone bridge there,
    Up to the ridge there :
  And,—it falling by chance,—

  " The Twenty-eighth led the van,
And skirmished all night as we lay there,—
As a tiger had fought for his prey there ;—
And so when the battle was ended
    In victory splendid,
  And man called unto man,

  " The voice of him, my own,
Made no response unto my bitter cry.
'O love,' I said, 'thou shalt not surely die ! '
But love was fled and troth was dead and he
    Came not to me !
  Yet love went not alone,—

  " The hand that bore the ring,
Symbol of plighted faith and deathless vow,
Lay ruddy with the seal of valor now,
And so it was I said, 'I pray thee take,
    E'en for Love's sake,
  This pledge whence visions spring

" ' Of souls dissevered wide,
Save for the fond allegiance that they owe
To home and country, for whose sake they know
Wounds, prisons, perils upon land and sea ;
   The grinning mockery
  Of smitten hope and pride.

" ' The exile from the face
Of wife, home, mother, aye, of all
The holy, happy names that we do call
The things which tell of heavy hearts grown light,
   And days made bright
  With Love's transforming grace.' "

So I gave back the ring ;
And saw her sadly, slowly turn away
Into wide streets where deepening shadows lay,
Loveless and lorn to pass wide open hall
   Where children call
  Who know no sorrowing ;

To see the eager twain,
Arm locked in arm, contented go
Into the light and life and warmth and glow ;

To hear the voice of laughter, and the sound
Of mirth around ;
And yet above her slain

To hush the love-lorn cry,
And glory in the valor that did go
Up to the cannon's mouth, up to the foe,
And would not for its own a portion take
E'en for Love's sake,
When men were called to die.

So Glory claims her own,—
Or be it on the rueful field of war,
Or by mute hearths where sorrow's ashes are ;
Where hearts are light and hearts are lcal,
Amid the clash of steel,
Where black-robed women moan !

These the Immortals love !
Theirs is the faith and fortitude that lead
To glorious sacrifice and valiant deed ;
Up to the shining citadel of Fame
Where each heroic name
Is writ in blood above !

AYE, BRING THE FADELESS EVER-GREENS.

Aye, bring the fadeless evergreens, the laurel and
the bay,
A grateful land remembers all her promises to-day;
And hearts that gave their treasures up when manhood was the price
Now bring their sweetest offerings and bless the
sacrifice.
It is no soulless pageantry o'er half forgotten
deeds
That draws from painted history the spirit of its
meeds !
In the pale and anxious faces that gather in the
crowd
Is found the brave sad story of the conquest and
the shroud.

Aye, bring the fadeless evergreens, the laurel and
the bay ;

They serve a nobler purpose now than under Ro-
    man sway ;
We'll twine them for our heroes with the cypress
    and the yew,
And weave them into garlands with the rosemary
    and rue.
The emblems of the conqueror, the emblems of the
    dead,
Shall rest, a silent homily, above each sleeping
    head ;
While victory is whispering of battles nobly won,
And peace runs after sorrow with her touching,
    tender tone.

Aye, bring the queen of flowers — the roses red and
    white—
Though we name no haughty Lancaster or York
    devoted knight,
We sing of grander deeds to-day, of greater battles
    won,
Of freemen wrapped in Freedom's flag when Free-
    dom's work was done.
Aye, strew the dew-wet roses — each liquid drop
    a tear

From eyes grown dim with weeping above the soldier's bier,—
For as their dying fragrance fills all the summer
morn,
So from the tomb of patriots is heroism born.

Aye, bring the pale white flowers, fresh and sweet
to look upon—
There are no purer symbols of the noble spirits
gone—
The fragrance floating from them comes to gladden
us to-day,
Like memories of cherished friends forever passed
away.
Aye, bring the stately flowers—the haughty *fleur
de lis*,
For never was it emblem of a truer royalty ;
To-day its crested head above a private's grave
may toss,
And yet no braver he who wore the helmet and the
cross.

Aye, come with flying banners and with stately mar-
tial tread !

With muffled drums and music gather 'round the
    honored dead !

And thus, with bowed heads standing, while we
    watch the maidens come

To strew our humble offerings on every sacred
    tomb—

And while the fires of sorrow burn in many a tear-
    less eye,

And hearts less used to grief bow down in speech-
    less agony ;—

Oh, will not then this earnest prayer arise to every
    tongue,

"God give to us such men as these, whatever trials
    come !"

THE BOYS OF MICHIGAN.

I sing the boys of Michigan, the hardy Wolverines,
The heroes of a hundred fights, a hundred war-like
scenes !
Full-armed they sprang to battle in the shock of
'sixty-one,
And turned no more for friend or foe till victory
was won.

To-day the forests echo as the ringing axes glide,
And the fisher shouts to fisher as they rock along
the tide ;
To-morrow, as the booms are swept adown the piney
streams,
In the bivouac of battle they dream the soldier's
dreams.

They rally to the East of us, they rally to the West,
With the ribbons and the roses knotted on each
manly breast ;

The ribbons and the roses that the hand of love has
    wrought,
In the splendor of the palace, in the humble forest
    cot.

From the mountains of Virginia comes the neighing
    of their steeds,
And the valor of the Union is emblazoned in their
    deeds ;
They ford the blue Potomac, they are camping by
    the James,
In the blood that courses heroes' veins they've writ
    their honored names.

On the shining Shenandoah, by the rippling Rapi-
    dan,
In the reckless raid with Stoneman, in the shock
    with Sheridan ;
Now at Fredericksburg with Burnside, now at Get-
    tysburg with Meade,
Where the hills of Pennsylvania resound to valiant
    deed.

'Twas but yesterday with Baxter, volunteers from
    rear to van,

8

That across the Rappahannock went the Seventh
    Michigan ;
On the swinging pontoon bridges, to the muzzles of
    the guns,—
Hurrah ! they sup in Fredericksburg, though red
    the river runs.

Like a meteoric shower trailing through the lurid
    night,
Come the troopers under Custer, spurred and booted
    for the fight ;
There is crashing of the cannon, and the angry mus-
    kets slay,
But the trooper's in the saddle and the torch is in
    his way.

In the West — God speed the battle ! — the Boys of
    Michigan
They are leading on with Sherman and with Thomas
    in the van ;
In the hells that hem Atlanta, in the marches to the
    sea,
They are shaking out the guidons that have made a
    Nation free !

Cheers for the Boys of Michigan ! Their work was
  nobly done,
For Grant's at Appomattox and the Rebel Chief
  out-run !
On the heights of lofty Lookout 'tis their banner we
  descry
Where the tempest of the valley smote the tempest
  of the sky.

Tears for the boys of Michigan, where'er their
  graves may be,
In the vales of old Virginia, on the hills of Tennessee !
Where the path of War lies beaten 'neath the fury
  of his wrath,
Where the spectres of the Prison keep the Nation's
  aftermath !

Cheers, cheers again, old comrades, brave sons of
  Michigan !
God bless you for the deeds you've done, God keep
  you to a man !
And cheers, brave hearts of Michigan ! Aye, three
  times three to-day
For that old flag for which you fought—our Na-
  tion's flag for aye !

THE BLACK REGIMENT AT PORT HUDSON.

"FORWARD, *double-quick, march!*"
  Through the smoke and the flame,
  Through the cyclone of shot and of shell;
  Seven times down the abyss,
  Seven times up to the guns,
  Shattered and scattered and scarred;
  The scourge at their head,
  And the scourge at their feet,
  Charged the Black Regiment.

  There on the heights were the guns,—
  The bloodhounds of battle,—
  The dark growling packs crouching low,
  To start at a word from the master,
  And roar and rend in the trail
  Of reeling disaster.
  Under the guns is the bayou,
  A marge of luxuriant grasses,—

And here are the tawny long lines,
Where the Orderly passes;
And their eyes are aflame,
As they charge and take aim,
Down where the bayou runs red
With the blood of the dead;
Where the snarer has set
The lines of his net;
And they sink and they fall
Beyond hope, beyond call,—
The gallant Black Regiment.

What did they down in the breach,
Under the guns at Port Hudson?
Slaves that they were and despiséd,
Scorned of the land and reviléd,—
Mocked at, and spit at, and spurnéd,—
Sold like an ox in the shambles,—
Torn from the breasts that would nurstle,
Hated and hunted and hurtled —
Who nerved their muscle,
Who strung their tendons?
Mother of freemen, give answer!

"Lo, while ye dozed in your tents
    With the languorous air

Blown soft from the gardens of musk
  Caressing you there,—
Your coraline lips,
  And your long silken hair,
And the pink waxen tips
  Of your fingers so fair,—
They toiled and grew strong
  In the gin and the cane,
And their ebony thighs,
  And their shoulders strong-knit,
For the Isthmian prize
  They were moulded and fit.
When they held up bruised hands
  Mine hastened to heal;
When they laid their lips close
  To my heart in the night,
I heard through their tears,
  And I taught them to feel
That who conquereth foes
  He must fight,—
    He must fight!"

  "*Forward, double-quick, march!*"
    The scoff and the jeer
      Are swift to pursue,

But the scoff and the jeer
  No hero may rue.
So steady and stiil
They stride down the hill,
Till the bloodhounds awake
On the brow of the brake,—
There to show their wide maws,
There to rend with fierce jaws,
While their clamor and blare
Cleave the pestilent air,—
And they rock and they reel
In the raging red wrath,
Though their hearts are as steel
There is death in the path,
And the knights of the seal,
They are keeping their math.

"*Forward, double-quick, march!*"
Though Nelson would stay
The long swinging lines
That are melting away,
In the dull, deadly glare
Of the war-wasting air,
Where the sun smites the head,

And the earth snares the feet,
And the lines that have led
Are the lines of defeat;
For the road to success
Is the road to despair,
And the toil and the stress
Reap but bitterness there.

"*Still forward, and charge for the guns!*"
Said Cailloux,
And his shattered sword-arm
Was the guidon they knew.
But a fire rakes the flanks
And a fire rakes the van;
He is down with the ranks
That go down as one man.

Shake the old colors out!
Planciancois ahead,—
Where he leads they follow,
Though the grave be their bed!
But the colors go down,
And the color-guard's slain,—
They bend 'neath the colors.
And forward again!

Through the shot and the shell,
 Through the gloom and the glare,
For the conquest lies here,
 And the glory lies there.
Alas for Planciancois !
 Alas for Cailloux !
For the heroes who fall
 In the ranks of the Blue!
For the gallant Black Regiment
 Under the guns
In the charge at Port Hudson !

What did they wrest from the breach
Under the guns at Port Hudson?
 From the rage of retreat,
 In the pangs of defeat?
 From the fury of hate,
 And the frenzy of fate ?
 From the jibe and the jeer,
 And the scorn and the sneer.
From revenge that leaps out
In the ruin and rout,
And gloats on the wounded,
 And gloats on the dead,

As the jackal that stirs
  The swift pulses of dread?

What did they wrest from the breach,
Under the guns at Port Hudson?
The right to be men; to stand forth
Clean-limbed in the fierce light of freedom,
And say, " *We are men!   We are men*
By these scars, by these wounds!" And what then?
" *Why, patriots, wed to our deeds,*
 In the face of the law and the creeds!
 By our flag ruby red
 With the blood of the dead,
 To stand by our land in her needs!
 The first of the fearless,
 The peer of the peerless,
 When glory to glory up-leads!"

Out of the awful abyss,
Up from the guns at Port Hudson,
Out of the smoke and the flame,
Shattered and scattered they came,—
  Casting the gyves of the slave,

Winning the gules of the free;
One on the rolls of the brave,
One in the glory to be,—
The gallant Black Regiment!

WELCOME HOME !

WELCOME ! welcome !   Hark ! the greeting
  From the glad home-voices comes,
Words which echo is repeating
  With the triumph-speaking drums.
Welcome home from fields of glory,
Sacred evermore in story,
Won by you in battles gory,—
      Welcome home !

Welcome ! welcome !   We remember
  When you proudly took the field ;
'T was the beautiful September,
  And the war-trumps loudly pealed.
Oh, how proud you seemed when passing
To the front, where troops were massing,
Loyal from disloyal classing,—
      Welcome home !

Welcome ! welcome !   We are thinking
  Of the wilds of Tennessee,

When with Burnside, all unshrinking,
  You assumed supremacy ;
And from then, your name maintaining,
Honors new and noble gaining,
Well you won the praise we're naming,—
    Welcome home !

Welcome ! welcome ! Ask of Sherman
  What of honor you may know !
He will answer, "Robes of ermine,
  Gold and gems, cannot bestow
Half the fame on those who wear them,
And in princely power bear them !"
Who with honor would compare them ?—
    Welcome home !

Welcome ! welcome ! Months have vanished
  Since on frowning Rocky Face
You all thoughts and feelings banished,
  Save to fill the hero's place.
Never were you seen retreating,
But the haughty foe defeating,
While the wildest storms were beating,—
    Welcome home !

Welcome ! welcome ! Those were battles
  Which the world is proud to name ;
Freeing all the human chattels,
  Filling traitor-hearts with shame.
Kenesaw's destructive charges,
Dallas and Lost Mountain's gorges,
Resaca—how the theme enlarges !—
    Welcome home !

Welcome ! welcome ! Hood surrounded
  And the fair Atlanta won,
Pæans through the Northland sounded
  For the good work you had done ;
And your great achievements summing,
In our hearts we said, "They're coming,
Hark ! the song of peace is humming !"—
    Welcome home !

Welcome ! welcome ! Darkness lowered
  Fearfully above us all,
When brave Thomas seemed o'erpowered,
  And his strength about to fall ;
But at Franklin, death defying,
While your comrades low were lying,
Back you sent the foemen flying,—
    Welcome home !

Welcome ! welcome ! We shall never
　　Cease to see the Nashville rout,
When with gleaming steel you ever
　　Made the rebels face about.
Hood's battalions are retreating,
Bugles blare and drums are beating,
Fame extends you royal greeting,—
　　　　Welcome home !

Welcome ! welcome ! We have shrined you
　　In the temple of our heart ;
And within it have entwined you
　　Fadeless wreaths with subtle art.
There are lines in Love's own letters,
Battles, prison-cells, and fetters ;
To your prowess we are debtors,—
　　　　Welcome home !

Welcome ! welcome ! God who kept you
　　All these weary days agone,
Though of comrades He bereft you,
　　He but gathered home His own ;
Ever guide you by His power,
Though the angry tempests lower,
Peace her blessings o'er you shower,—
　　　　Welcome home !

Welcome ! welcome ! For the sleeping
   Heroes in their distant graves,
We the silent tears are weeping,
   While their blood-bought banner waves ;
But its sacred folds can never
Treason lift a hand to sever,
Clasp we hands, then, and forever ! —
   Welcome home !

CHRISTMAS AT THE SOLDIERS' ORPHANS' HOME.

THE Christmas morn was breaking ; and startled from my sleep
By merry chimes in chorus and joy-bells loud and deep,
I breathed a hurried matin, and, turning round my head,
The brightest forms and faces came dancing to my bed.

I looked up quite bewildered, and puzzled much to say
If on the earth, or fairies had stolen me away ;
For beaming black eyes dazzled, and laughing blue eyes shone,
And with the radiant vision mine eyes had blinded grown.

And O the flaxen ringlets and curls of sunny brown.

9

That over dimpled faces and shoulders rippled
  down ;
And O the silvery voices that rang through house
  and hall—
" A merry, merry Christmas ! A merry Christmas
  all ! "

But even more I marveled — for mingling in the
  shout
Were words of foreign meaning I could not well
  make out,—
"*St. Nicholas*," "*Kris Kringle*," and "*Santa Claus*,"
  I heard,
With " *Pelschnicol*," " *Knecht Rupert*," and many
  another word.

Among the merry dancers was happy little Nell,
And all her darling playmates from near and far as
  well,
In floating white, with sashes of blue and pink and
  red,
And full of fun and frolic was every little head.

And little people, oddest of any ever seen,
Tripped merrily in quaintest of costumes gray and
  green,

The skirts of some were trailing, and some cut at
the knee,
And on their feet were sandals and buskins queer
to see.

One wore a gown of linsey, a 'kerchief round her
neck,
And wooden shoes, and close-set cap, and apron
made of check ;
And beckoning unto me the modest little miss,
I said, "*Meine Fraulein*, tell me who your Kris
Kringle is ! "

Then modestly the maiden told in her simple
phrase,
Of dear Kris Kringle going through broad and
narrow ways,
To burgher and to cotter as to the mighty king,
And leaving all good children some pretty, dainty
thing.

How on the Christmas even he hangs the lighted
tree,
With toys, and brightest ribbons, and flowers fair to
see ;

And how when *Kinder* gather with glad and smiling
eyes,
Knecht Rupert showers candies and laughs at their
surprise.

Then came a dimpled darling in linen bib and hose,
And cheeks and lip, I'm certain, as red as any rose ;
Then I : " O merry maiden of merry England, say
What do ye in your country on merry Christmas
day ? "

" We gather in the holly with scarlet berries bright,
We hang the sacred mistletoe and dance by the
Yule-fire light ;
We pass the steaming wassail with ribbons round
the bowl,
While merry Christmas carols from hall to cottage
roll.

"And with the bright-leaved holly we gather in
good-will,
And with the sacred mistletoe we banish every ill,
And in the smoking wassail drown enmity and
strife,
And in the tender carol call blessings on our life.

" And then the mighty pudding stuffed full of juicy
　　plums,
And rare mince pie and cider, and rusk and white-
　　bread crumbs,
And far into the midnight the feasting and the
　　games,—
The only night when wee folk have any sort of
　　claims."

A lad in kilt and plaidie came bravely up and
　　talked
About the masqueraders that in his country stalked,
Disguised in strangest costumes, with horns and
　　pipes and wigs,
And danced the reel and hornpipe and lilting High-
　　land jigs.

A youth from France the sunny came singing Notre
　　Dame,
How people wreathe the altars with garlands, and
　　the balm
Of charities and flowers and words of kindly cheer
Become sweet consecration for each new Christmas
　　year.

"What word, O brown Italian?" With dark and
    flashing eye,
And floating robe of crimson he softly glided by,
And many glowing pictures of good St. Nicholas
    drew,
Who comes each year to Florence, and Rome, and
    _ Venice too ;

And brings good gifts and gladness to humble
    hearth and home,
And rings the merry revels from lofty minster-dome,
And fills the streets with people, their hearts with
    holy fire,
And sings the grand old anthems in proud St.
    Peter's choir.

And from remotest countries and further ocean
    isles,
Wherever Christ is worshipped, they came with songs
    and smiles ;
In robes of fur from Russia, in silk from far Siam,
The Laplander in muffler, the Hindoo with his fan.

And in one mighty chorus they sang a holy hymn,
About the Christ-Child dwelling in far-off Bethle-
    hem,

Till in a cloud of glory I saw them float away,
Like stars that softly vanish with the coming of the
    day.

But still the anthem lingered through all the Christ-
    mas morn,
The song I think the angels sung when Christ the
    Lord was born ;
When, bending o'er the manger, the prophets hailed
    their King,
And in the lap of Mary poured precious offering.

Now God be thanked, who gave us this day of all
    the days,
When hand in hand the nations extol His matchless
    ways !
Ring out, glad bells, the story, the gladdest of the
    year !
Sing out, glad souls, your carols, till earth and
    heaven hear !

CHARGE OF THE MAINE REGIMENTS.

WHERE Rappahannock's waters roll
　　Adown Virginia's wasted plain,
Where seaward dash its troubled waves
　　To mingle with the angry main,
Brave Sedgwick with his gallant corps,
　　His war-bronzed corps of valiant men,
Marched proudly o'er the blood-stained way,
　　To meet the sturdy foe again.
" Charge for the guns, boys ! charge ! " he cried :
　" Charge for your homes, your firesides free !
Charge for your country's life and pride !
　　Charge for the boon of liberty ! "
Then, dashing on, through shot and shell,
They nobly fought, or nobly fell.

First to storm the frowning earthworks,
　　Rushed the Sixth and Seventh Maine ;
While the whizzing balls and bullets
　　Showered down like autumn rain,

On firm hands that trembled never,
  On true hearts that would not quail ;
There was no weak arm to shudder,
  No false voice to whisper "*Fail.*"
Twice they charged in quick succession,
  Twice, through galling murderous fire,
Twice repulsed, both horse and footman
  Sought again the conflict dire ;
Till, every leader lying slain,
Alone they raised the flag again.

And gathering 'neath its shining folds,
  They said, while smiled its cheering stars,
" Boys, let us charge again, and hold
  The works without our officers.
We'll bravely on, nor halt, nor turn ;
  What though we fall ? we triumph still,
For every drop of blood we shed
  Shall raise a host our ranks to fill.
On, then ! on, o'er the crimson field !
On ! on ! through the blood of the slain !
On ! on ! and the battlements gain
Heaven shall catch a gladsome strain ;
For joining we will send on high,
To God, our praise for victory."

Then on they sped, while cannons raged,
　　And belched their fury o'er their way,
Till on the works their banners waved
　　Through battle smoke that dimmed the day.
O Rappahannock! gently roll
　　Your moaning billows to the sea;
And ever let your murmured dirge
　　Rise upward for the fallen free;
For those who, filled with holy zeal,
　　With love of country half divine,
Gave all their cherished hopes and joys,
　　As offerings for their country's shrine.
Then gently, river, roll your waves;
Your banks are lined with sacred graves.

THE BOY HERO'S MOTHER.

STRICKEN heart that throbs with grief,
By the waves of sorrow tossed,
Mourning for the early lost,—
    Look above !
Hopes now wrecked upon the reef
Shall revive in endless love ;—
    Look above !

Spirit bowed with crushing woe,
Light the darkest gloom enshrouds;
Penetrate the battle clouds !—
    Look above !
Triumph follows Freedom's blow,
Sent from realms of endless love ;—
    Look above !

Canst thou pierce the heavy gloom ?
Canst thou clasp the promise sealed
Righteous truth can never yield !—
    Look above !

'Round your hero's lowly tomb,
Glows the light of endless love ; —
　Look above !

Young in years but strong in zeal,
Could he stand inactively
By the flag of Liberty ? —
　Look above !
Immortality shall seal
All his deeds in endless love ; —
　Look above !

He, to right his country's wrong,
In the priceless hours of youth
Grasped the mighty sword of truth ; —
　Look above !
And, with soul-triumphant song,
Soared to realms of endless love ; —
　Look above !

Higher service there is none
Than to save our Fatherland
From a vaunting traitor-band ; —
　Look above !

Glory claims him for her own,
Twines his brow in endless love ; —
   Look above !

One more sacrifice is given,
One more home is robbed of light,
Dwelling now in deepest night ; —
   Look above !
Sacred ties on earth are riven ;
But abide in endless love ; —
   Look above !

Waiting spirit, crushed and torn,
Drinking yet the cup of gall,
Or hast drained its marah all, —
   Look above !
Soon beyond earth's sorrows borne
Thou shalt dwell in endless love ! —
   Look above !

TOAST OF THE IRISH VOLUNTEER.

WHEN the Red, White and Blue was lowered
    before us,
And trailed in the dust by an insolent foe,
When treacherous tongues in their threatening
    chorus
Avowed it should e'er in dishonor lay low,
        The bravest and best
        Clasped its folds to their breast,
And swore to uplift it in glory again.
        Then foremost were seen
        The sons of the Green ;
Their hands they had laid on their new country's
    altar,
Whose freedom had wooed them from Erin away,
In the Army and Navy, ah ! when did they falter ?
Their praise is well sung on St. Phadrig's Day.

On mount Croagh Phadrig, the saint in whose favor
    Each Irish heart struggles to dwell in the while

Spake words of such weight as to banish forever
  The plagues that infested his beautiful isle.
      A careful gleaning
      Imparts us the meaning
That vices and wrongs were the evils he fought ;
      A faint repetition
      Of the honored tradition
We recently had in our own favored land,
  When the grossest of crimes was wiped quite away
By our " Army and Navy," which ever will stand
  A time-honored toast on St. Phadrig's Day.

Then long wave the Green ! it shall float with our
      colors,
  Since 'neath the Old Flag those who loved it have
    .   died ;
Their hearts were with ours in our season of
      dolors,
  They shall still be with ours in the hour of our
      pride.
      So shall the sweet song
      Of triumph belong
To the loyal and leal, be their clime what it will.
      The Green and the White,
      The Blue and the Bright,

Shall harmonize well in their kindred communion,
  And flash into light though the morning be gray ;
And the " Army and Navy," the pride of the Union,
  Be first on the toasts of St. Phadrig's Day.

THE WELCOME GRAVE.

THROUGH all the long night, from the left to the
right
  The war-cries of Freedom had pealed ;
But we watched on our arms, till the battle alarms
  Had summoned us forth to the field.
In the thick wooded gorge we prepared for the
charge,
  Strong and firm, not a battle-line swayed.
" On, and victory reap, on the rock-bounded steep!"
  Said our chief ; not a man was dismayed.
          Where our brave banner waves,
We will follow it well through the shot and the
shell,
          Though to patriot graves.

Then we rushed on the foe, in an unbroken row,
  That beautiful morning in June ;
While cheer after cheer, from the front to the rear,
  Swept down through the open lagune ;
          10

The queen of the night, in her swift-going flight,
Had crossed o'er that white-tented lea ;
And dropping her gems, decked the leaf-enriched
stems
Of every flower and tree.
.   And the azure-hued skies
Kissed the fresh-growing earth into gladness and
mirth,
Like a new Paradise.

But for us not the sweet of the woodland retreat—
Our orders, to conquer or die !
So we proudly advanced, while the bright sunshine
danced
On our arms like a smile from on high ;
Then they poured on our ranks from the opposite
banks
The death-dealing missiles of war.
When a shell with a scream, and a quick angry
gleam,
Sunk down like an ill-omened star.
And our hearts throbbed with pain,
As we sighed for the braves doomed to cold lonely
graves,
On that desolate plain.

'Twas a swift passing thought, and we poured the
    red shot
    And turned the cold steel on the foe.
Though they massed in their strength, they fell
    broken at length,
    Or fled to their strongholds below.
And we rested a pace from the wearisome chase,
    And gazed o'er the crimson-stained field,
Where the brave-hearted dead had their sacred
    blood shed,
    And by the death-angel were sealed.
          While away to the right
Were bits of the shell which so wrathfully fell ;
          But no victims in sight.

Can worldly cares save in the peace of the grave ?
    Can conflict its quiet molest ?
And anguish—ah no ! so securely below,
    From carnage, the hero found rest.
Not the calm peaceful rest which the perfectly blest
    In the dreamless Forever have gained,
But a refuge from harm, which the triumphant arm
    Of the angel of battle had deigned ;

And in wonder we spoke,
For we felt in that hour the sovereign power
Of the aid we invoke.

The pickets who stood at the edge of the wood
In the dawn of the morning had seen
The dark forms of men emerged from the glen,
Through the white mists that gathered between ;
Then as suddenly halt where the blue smiling
vault
Of Heaven seemed close through the trees.
"We will bury him here, where the fragrant flowers
near
Will lavish their sweets on the breeze."
And they scooped a rude grave,
Ah ! above their wild dream, a power supreme
Through them purposed to save.

Ah ! we seem not to know that deep-hidden below
Our plans, are the workings divine
Of the spirit of light sent to guide us aright,
And justice with mercy combine.
And forget that the eye which afar from the
sky
Can see e'en the poor sparrow fall,

Will endless watch keep, though we thoughtlessly
    sleep,
    And guide us through fears that appall ;
        And when dangers have grown
So thick at our feet that there seems no retreat,
        He will bear up His own.

COMRADESHIP.

HAND in hand we wander,
Through the world together
In the sunny weather,
   In the chilling showers;
And what time we squander
In our simple pleasures,
We reclaim in treasures
   From the working hours.

We have often tarried
In the fragrant meadows,
Or the grateful shadows
   Of the silent wood;
And the storms have parried,
Clinging closer ever,
Did the lightnings sever
   Where we startled stood.

We have wanted little
Since the hour we started;
Very hopeful-hearted

Have we ever gone ;
Though the merest tittle
Of the world's good treasure
Could we ever measure
     For ourselves alone.

There are harder lessons
In a life to vex one
Than the pressing question
     Of our daily bread ;
But the swift impressions
Of a willing spirit
Are the hands of merit
     Spinning fortune's thread.

And it little matters
Where our earthly lot is,
If our only thought is
     To be happy there ;
For the Sower scatters
Good in evil places,
And the true heart traces
     Blessings everywhere.

TWENTY YEARS AGO.

1865–1885.

I STAND and count the flying years upon my fingers,
    thus :

Five, ten, fifteen, and twenty,—an age it seems to us

Since, flinging down our haversacks, unstripping belt
    and gun,

We bade good-bye to want and war that day at
    Washington.

The bronze was in our faces and the sheen was in
    our eyes,

Though the fighting had been awful, boys,—this
    fact we can't disguise ;

But we strode with sturdy paces, and our hearts
    were all aglow,

For Youth and Love they beckoned us—just twenty
    years ago.

Now, we scan each others' faces to see if we can tell

'Neath bleaching locks, the boyish traits we learned
    to love so well,

Or can tell the slender comrade, the rollicking, the
    gay,
In that doughty dignitary who steps so slow to-day;
To learn if live the gallant boys who laughed at
    Rebel lead,
If there were any foes to fight, or any fun ahead,
Who knew the sign and countersign, and gave the
    quick hollo,
When prowling round the picket-line—yes, twenty
    years ago.

And how have gone the years with you, O comrades
    tried and true,
Since laying down the musket and casting off the
    blue?
And where is pitched your bivouac? Who messes
    with you now?
And are you training new recruits to toe the mark?
    And how
Are rations with you, comrades? What, a little
    short, you say?
Though you forage late and early, your prizes slip
    away?

But you camp in snugger quarters, aye, comrades,
    this we know,
Than when wrapped within your blankets—more
    than twenty years ago.

Hark! hark! Yon mighty rumbling! Again and
    yet again !
What mean those angry echoes in the piney woods
    of Maine ?
"Tis not the rolling tempest, the crash of rudders
    dashed
Against the grinding granite, the forelands ocean-
    lashed !
'Tis not the wrath of earthquakes come creeping
    through the seas,
From the ragings of Vesuvius, the battered walls
    of Greece !
Boom ! boom ! The valleys tremble, the hills are
    rocking low :
It is the blast of Battle—four-and-twenty years ago !

Boom ! boom ! The guns of Sumter are thundering
    at our doors,
Above the beetling breakers the tide of battle pours ;

The oath of War is spoken, from mouth to mouth
    it runs,—
And over in Skowhegan the women man the guns.
Boom! boom! It is the call for me, it is the call for
    you !
Boom! boom! for men of mettle to don the Union
    blue ;
The long-roll it is sounding, it wakened with a blow
The bivouac of ages—four-and-twenty years ago !

Swing out your flags, O comrades, and keep your
    paces true,
For Freedom calls for valiant men when she has
    work to do !
Lo, there are mothers praying and wives to speak
    " Good cheer,"
And there are children pleading — God grant the
    end be near !
And there are comrades dying, their whispers thrill
    us yet,—
O mute and mournful memories we never can
    forget !
" *Go, tell her that her flag and mine I saved ere
    stricken low,—*"

Ah, comrades ! sad the messages of twenty years
  ago !

Let others sing the songs of War: we sing the
  songs of Peace ;
The splendors of the battle pale before such thoughts
  as these ;
For ours was not the march of hate, of devastating
  band,
To set the falcons of despoil a-flying through the
  land ;
We knew no braggart boast of arms, we had no
  wish to roam,
Our feet sped on where duty called, our hearts were
  still at home ;
On weary march, in dreary camp, our ranks were
  all aglow,
If but the mails a letter brought — aye, twenty
  years ago.

O comrades, hand-in-hand upon the headland heights
  of Maine—
The State that never lost a flag, that never charged
  in vain,—

What see you on the Westward line ? What see
    you at the South,
Where June is wreathing roses within the cannon's
    mouth ?
What see you there at Gettysburg ? The brooding
    wings of Love,
The violets a-blowing the Blue and Gray above !
Span mountain unto mountain, link vale to vale,
    and lo,
It is the Arch of Peace we fashioned twenty
    years ago !

O Nation great, State linked to State in bonds that
    none can break,
From Ocean unto Ocean, from Gulf to Northern
    lake !
State linked to State, fate linked to fate, in mart
    and mint and mine,
In rolling plain of golden grain, in toss of plumy
    pine !
State linked to State in goodly fate that sounds the
    swift advance,
Where banners that have wooed the world before
    our legions dance !

This is the dream that crowns our years; and when
  our heads are low,
Float out, float on, O Union flag, as twenty years
  ago !

PART II.

OTHER POEMS.

PRISCILLA, AQUILA, AND PAUL.

METHOUGHT on Corinth's citadel
  I gazed far down the strand,
Where, twice a thousand feet below,
  The fair fleets sail and land ;
And half across the Isthmian plain
  The mountain shadows chase
And clasp a thousand domes and towers
  Within their close embrace.

I looked; and lo, three other forms
  Beside me on the wall :
Priscilla one, Aquila one,
  And one the saintly Paul.

They stood and viewed the stately ships
  Come back from Tyre and Rome,
The black-prowed argosies from Ind
  Bear gold and spices home ;
I saw them scan the western shores
  Where high Parnassus shines,

11

Above the Delphian oracles,
  Above the Delphian shrines.

" O Christ, be pitiful to these ! "
  They said, both one and all:
Priscilla one, Aquila one,
  And one the saintly Paul.

Unto the East I saw them turn,
  And gaze with wondering eyes,
Where, gleaming on the Athenian heights,
  Minerva's altars rise ;
Where, on the bay, fair Athens lifts
  Her temples to the sun,
And, thither pointing, Paul relates
  The mighty works there done ;
How on the summit of Mars' Hill,
  Beneath Minerva's throne,
He mocked the wrath of all the gods,
  Proclaiming ONE UNKNOWN.

They bowed their heads and blessed His
      name
  Who loves both great and small :
Priscilla one, Aquila one.
  And one the saintly Paul.

Below us the Saronic gulf
   Lay dimpling in the sun,
Her fertile islands reaching down
   Unto the fair Colonne ;
To right of us Lepanto laughs
   Beside the Sicyon shore ;
And all between, the olive yards,
   And vineyards purpling o'er,
And lemon groves, and citron,
   And orange rows and corn,
And cyprus for the Isthmian crowns
   Of heroes newly born.

"*It is a plenteous land and fair,*"
   They spake, both one and all :
Priscilla one, Aquila one,
   And one the saintly Paul.

There, Neptune's mighty colonnades
   Above the Stadium rise,
Where Greece sends down her knightliest
      youths
   To struggle for the prize ;
And there, upreaching step by step,
   The Theatre of stone,

And hugging close the Isthmic wall
  The tower of Palæmon.
It is a goodly sight, I ween,
  This city of two seas—
A queen between two lovers set—
  The citadel of Greece.

"*May Christ pour out his spirit here*,"
  They prayed, both one and all:
Priscilla one, Aquila one,
  And one the saintly Paul.

Then spake the great Apostle:
  "Across yon liquid blue
There rise as glorious cities
  As any now we view;
As precious to that Saviour
  Who said, ' *Go, tell of me*
Unto all climes and kingdoms
  In lands beyond the sea.'
Now ye, most wise Priscilla,
  And Aquila, go with me;
That even there at Ephesus,
  As here at Corinth, we

May name the name of Jesus
  Where great Diana's shrined,
Till the ashes of her temples
  Shall be scattered with the wind."

I heard the twain take up their vows
  Unto the solemn call:
Priscilla one, Aquila one,
  And one the saintly Paul.

And now from busy Cenchrea,
  Fair Corinth's strong right arm,
Where Phebe and the brethren give
  A God-speed, sad but warm,—
Across the Ægean waters blue,
  Among her thousand isles,
They sail, and sail, until beyond
  The Ephesian harbor smiles
Diana's glittering colonnade
  Reflecting back the sun
From capitols and cornices
  And friezes one by one.

And there from house to house they taught
  The people one and all:

Priscilla one, Aquila one,
  And one the saintly Paul.

O Paul ! beneath thy rods and stripes,
  In perils on the deep,
In perils from an hundred ills
  That slumber not nor sleep,
In weariness and watchings,
  In hungerings oft, and thirst,
In nakedness, in agony,
  From unbelief accursed,
How blessed in such love to share,
  Such home thy home to call,—
Priscilla one, Aquila one,
  And one the saintly Paul.

God only knoweth all they wrought
  In that Ephesian town—
Priscilla and Aquila
  Belovèd in renown ;
Now toiling on with busy hands,
  Now jeopardizing all,
Instructors of Apollos,
  Co-laborers with Paul ;

God only knoweth how at Rome
  They cheered the martyr's heart,
Now ready to be offered
  In that clamorous Roman mart.

Methinks the three together walked
  Beyond that city's wall :
Priscilla one, Aquila one,
  And one the saintly Paul.

At Rome, upon the Ostian way
  Caius Cestus' tomb
Still lifts its lofty cenotaph
  Above the surrounding gloom ;
And thence down all the centuries
  Has come the Martyr's plea :
" *Priscilla greet, Aquila greet,*
  Ye churches yet to be ! "

They bore his body thence with tears,
  When he had suffered all :
Priscilla one, Aquila one,—
  And one the martyred Paul.

Again on Corinth's mount I stand
  And view the lands below :

The idol temples in the dust
   Are crumbled long ago ;
And where the three together stood
   A thousand thousand stand,
And sail and sail to golden shores
   Beyond the Ephesian strand.

But still we hear the voice of Paul
   Unto all people call:
" *Priscilla greet, Aquila greet,*
   That Christ be all in all."

THE COMING OF THE MAY.

With the early dawn I'm waking,
    And joy is in the air ;
The song of birds is breaking
    The silence everywhere ;
And my heart is full of longing
    I cannot all allay,
In dear old haunts to welcome
    The coming of the May.

In those rare enchanted orchards
    Where peach and apple bloom
Are filling all the long bright hours
    With delicate perfume,
Or within the grand old forests
    Where sun and shadow play,
'Twere very sweet again to greet
    The coming of the May.

There are such countless treasures
    In forests far away—

The starry-eyed anemones,
  And lady-slippers gay;
And I can tell the very spot
  Where orchids hide away
Their pretty precious faces
  Till the coming of the May.

I know just where the violets
  Bloom in the meadow hedge,
And where the pink arbutus trails
  Adown the river ledge;
Where trilliums and blue-bells low
  Are bowing all the day,
To welcome with their dainty grace
  The coming of the May.

And the slopes upon the hilltops
  Where grows the mountain tea,
Where sassafras and birch abound,
  Are known so well to me;
And the bends of brook and river
  Where trout and turtle stay,
And mussel-shells gleam whitely
  In the coming of the May.

Where the robin is a-singing,
  'Twere joy again to go—
I've heard sometimes a music
  In the cawing of the crow—
Where the bobolink is trilling
  His merry roundelay,
For all glad things are gladder
  In the coming of the May.

Yet I, my feet returning
  To childhood's haunts again,
Might find them very barren
  And strangely full of pain ;
The forms that wandered with me
  Would be shadows in the way,
And my heart might e'en be heavy
  In the coming of the May.

But, with earnest, eager longing
  I cannot well define,
I'm turning to the meadows,
  The woods of birch and pine.
Ah Memory, be kind to me !
  Let all else fade away,
But spare my heart its rapture
  In the coming of the May !

SWEET CHARITY.

THREE stately forms rode down the street,
　Rode down on palfreys three :
And one was Faith, and one was Hope,
　And one was Charity.

And Faith, upon her blood-red steed,
　Was girt with bow and spear ;
And Hope her charger dark as night
　Urged on with words of cheer.

But bending o'er a snowy mane
　There beamed most graciously
The saintly face and saintly smile
　Of blessed Charity.

"Come ride with me," now one and all,
　They spake with one accord ;
And Faith cried, "Don your panoply,"
　And Hope held out reward.

But bending from her milk-white steed,
   A voice came soft to me
And said, "My child, you're sick and sore;
   Come ride with Charity."

She drew me to her saddle bow
   And clasped me with a smile,
And pressed unto her heart we rode
   Through many a weary mile ; —

Through bands of fierce and boisterous men,
   With garments dashed with blood ;
Through noisy streets, and angry marts,
   And charges like a flood.

And Faith urged on the mighty men
   Who fight with spear and bow,
And Hope the holy men who do
   The joy of giving know.

But Charity stooped down to lift
   The beggar to his feet,
And in her train a weary host
   Of pilgrim souls to greet.

We rode until we came unto
  A gleaming jasper gate,—
There Faith flings down her battered shield,
  And all expectant wait.

The gleaming gate is open swung,
  And lo, an angel see,
Who sweetly calls: " Now welcome Faith,
  And Hope, and Charity!

" And who are these ye bring to me
  From that far world and drear ? "
And Faith said: " Lo, the saints who strove
  To gain an entrance here."

And Hope with radiant smile spake out :
  " Behold the godly men
Who for the rich rewards have deemed
  Their fifty years as ten."

But Charity said: " These are they
  Whose lives were lone and sad ;
No joy had they in striving,
  And no rewards they had."

The jasper gates were opened wide,
  They entered great and small ;
And Faith upon her blood-red steed
  Stood guard beside the wall.

And Hope with face uplifted
  Extended beckoning hand
Unto the distant pilgrims
  Who sought the golden land.

But midst the throng expectant,
  The milk-white steed alone
Strode through the gates of jasper
  Unto the great white throne.

Then from the veil of splendor
  A voice was heard to say:
" All hail thou well-belovéd,
  Thou hast been long away ! "

When from the milk-white palfrey
  The gracious rider sprung,
I saw the hands were piercéd
  To which I'd fondly clung.

And thus I know if Heaven's gate
  Shall ope for you and me,
'Twill be through God's Incarnate Love
  We name sweet Charity.

MARGUERITE.

LIKE a glad bride asleep
    In robes of white,
Earth smiles ; and yet I keep
    Sad watch to-night,—
Saying, "Marguerite,
Ma petite Marguerite,
When in that fair, far country shall we meet,
    Marguerite ?"

I waken with the dawn
    And say, " Her eyes
Look from wide windows on
    The dear South-skies,
Where, calling, 'Marguerite,
Ma petite Marguerite,'
She flung white oleanders at my feet,
    Marguerite !"

O fair child of the sun,
    Can I say, Come,

Where skies are chill and dun?
My heart grows dumb!
Oh, speak, Marguerite,
Ma petite, Marguerite,
Can love make all climes beautiful and sweet,
Marguerite?

O FRIEND OF MINE.

My thoughts to thee, O friend of mine,
    Are ever going,
Like the glad rills that, singing through the pine,
    Are swiftly flowing;
    Bearing the soft perfume
    Of fir and lily bloom,
      Unto the river,
    And with a thousand sweets,
    From love-enthroned retreats
      Enamored quiver.

My life with thine, O friend of mine,
    Is surely blending—
Like the glad rill that, singing from the pine
    Finds joyful ending.
    Oh, that the kindly sun
    Would keep us two in one,
      Love-bound forever!
    Oh, that the kindly breeze,
    Would kiss us to the seas,
      Parted, oh, never!

TURN O'ER A NEW LEAF.

THE last page you've written is crumpled and
      blurred,
  The prints of soiled fingers are plain ;
Your letters misshapen, your syllables slurred,
  Show the copy was followed in vain ;
But pray do not lift a disconsolate face,
  Nor yield to a profitless grief,
But gather fresh courage, look shame in the face—
    Turn o'er a new leaf !

How shining and bright ! How spotless and pure !
  How plain is the copy to view !
Now steady and slow ! As you start you are sure
  The rest of your task to pursue.
The Master stands near ; He will come at your call,
  If perchance you may need His relief ;
His voice it is speaking to one and to all—
    "Turn o'er a new leaf !"

WATCHING FOR ME AT THE WINDOW.

WATCHING for me at the window
  Through ringlets of flossy gold,
With the roses clasped in his fingers
  As only a child may hold ;
And his eyes like the laughing bluebells
  That dance in the dusky wold.

Watching for me at the window,
  O sweetest of baby boys,
Forgetting his gleesome frolic,
  Forgetting his treasured toys !
O rarest of budding roses,
  O dearest of earthly joys !

Watching for me at the window ;
  But oh, it is far and high,
And my feet they are weary of climbing
  Since my darling no longer is nigh ;
With his eyes that are glad at my coming,
  And his voice that responds to my cry.

Watching for me at the window,
　O darling, I hasten to thee,
As up from the din of the city
　In the days I may nevermore see ;
To clasp thee again to my bosom,
　In the Heaven that waits for me.

A NEW YEAR'S WISH.

ACROSS the solemn spaces of the years
How sweet to hear the voices that we knew
When life had less of sorrows than of tears,
And fewer hearts were sad and more were true!
Then take we gladder hope to us again,—
For who shall say that all our past is vain,
While one sweet soul esteems our little worth,
And singles us from all the good of earth
For kindly greeting as the days go by?
O friend of mine, whose rare fidelity
Stands sentinel at Friendship's holy shrine,
Lest care and change dissever souls at one,
The Lord keep watch between us, mine and thine,
Till night is gone and golden dawn begun!

STARRY WITNESSES.

On the hill and in the green,
  Through the dewy meadow,
Underneath the feet of men,
  In the sun and shadow,
Lo, she lifteth up her face
  To each rival comer,—
Dandelion, crown and grace
  Of the perfect Summer.

Who hath sent thee, starry one,
  With thy faith and meekness,
And thy lessons to out-run
  Thoughts of human weakness?
Who hath set thee in the way
  Of the faint and weary,
Just to teach that beauty may
  Bloom where all is dreary?

Who hath said : "O flower, go
  To my sons and daughters,

Tell them there is room to grow,
  Down by many waters;
That if crowded from the plain
  To the lane and by-way,
They may lift their heads again,
  Brave as on the highway."

There is One who knoweth well
  Human hearts are breaking,
Knoweth more than we can tell
  Of their silent aching:
And along the rugged ways
  Tender tokens giveth;
Starry witnesses give praise
  That Our Father liveth.

WOOD VIOLETS.

VIOLETS, my violets,
  Springing from the mould,
From the star-grass and the mosses
  Of the woodland dim and old ;
Sweet the stories you are telling
  Of the fading, happy years,
When the loves were young that vanished
  Long ago in mists and tears.

Violets, my violets,
  Gazing, I a moment go
Where the moist sweet woody odors
  All around me breathe and blow ;
Where the bluebells dip their clusters,
  And the purple orchids hide ;
And, with heart grown strangely happy,
  Fling my burdens all aside.

Violets, my violets,
  There was once a child that flew

Through the depths of field and forest,
　Searching patiently for you ;
And that child who now so wearies
　Of the fairest thing that grows,
Once grew wild with rapture finding
　But a single woodland rose.

Violets, my violets,
　If you knew how dark and chill
All our fair young world is growing,
　Could you bloom so lovely still?
Could you waken hopes that, flying,
　Swiftly fall with broken wings,
If you knew a time of dying
　Stills the sweetest voice that sings?

Violets, my violets,
　It is but a little boon :
Bend your kindly eyes above me,
　When I go, or late, or soon;
And perchance some sad one going
　Through the forests of the dead,
Shall remember where I'm sleeping,
　By the violets at my head.

THE OLD GNARLED APPLE-TREE.

OF all the childish memories
  That brighten with the flying years,
And bring a gladness to the eyes
  Like laughter coming after tears,
There's none that makes the heart bound on
  With all its youthful jollity,
Like that sweet vision of the lawn—
  The old gnarled apple-tree.

It stood just where the lawn swept down
  Into a rapid, steep descent,
Beneath each stately neighbor's frown,
  A placid picture of content;
And let the years bring what they would,
  The orchards bare or burdened be,
Abundant fruit it bore and good—
  The old gnarled apple-tree.

'Twas said that many years agone
  A sad-faced lady, with her child,
Came unattended and alone,
  And dwelt within the western wild;
She by the simple people round
  Was more than human deemed to be;
Her saintly hand placed in the ground
  The old gnarled apple-tree.

The woman seemed half happy grown;
  The child was desolate and sad,
The flowers and the birds had flown—
  The only playmates that he had;
And so one day, in wanton play,
  He ran with rude and reckless glee;
One tender sapling broken lay—
  The old gnarled apple-tree.

The woman bound it with a tear,
  And blessed it in her saintly way;
And that is why from year to year,
  As I have heard the people say,
The springtime always brings her bloom,
  The summer fruitage fair to see,

To crown with plenty and perfume
  The old gnarled apple-tree.

All glad things loved the dear old tree ;
  And early came the screaming jay
The robin and the honey-bee,
  And children laughing in the way ;
And in the dawn and in the dew
  Arose a joyous melody—
The praiseful song of Nature to
  The old gnarled apple-tree.

My little sister, fair and sweet,—
  Now sadly far from me, alas ! —
'Twas only yesterday our feet
  Slipped softly through the dewy grass ;
Slipped through the grass, and through the gloom,
  And wild with merriment and glee
We filled our wide-spread aprons from
  The old gnarled apple-tree !

Do I but wander? When alone
  My life grows young and glad and warm ;
The dearest joys the heart has known
  Are void of earthly shape and form.

Then fly, my soul, and clasp again
The sacred sweets of memory!
The fondest loves of youth enchain
The old gnarled apple-tree!

A FRIEND'S SOUVENIR.

YOUR little gift-box, dear, I own,
  With all the treasures in it;
But fairer far the face that shone
  On me one little minute —
That glad and gracious face that makes
  The dimmest place seem cheery,
And takes away a thousand aches
  From hearts grown sick or weary.

I do remember how a hand
  Stole tenderly unto me,
One hour when care's acute command
  Had sent a shiver through me;
I do remember how that thrill
  Of speechless consolation
Keeps all my pulses bounding still
  In silent exaltation.

Sweet friend, thy beauty is of God,
  To bless and cheer and brighten;

A bounteous sun to fling abroad
  The hopes that help and lighten ;
Thy heart a well-spring full and strong
  A fount of generous feeling ;
Thy soul a happy bird of song
  Toward which our loves are stealing.

WHAT DO THE ROSES SAY?

WHAT do the roses say, love, my love,
   Glad as the morning and fair as the South?
Bend to me fondly the rose-red leaves
   Of your rose-red mouth!

What do the roses say, sweet, my sweet,
   Light as the zephyrs and bright as the dawn?
Summer is beckoning, youth is fleet,
   Let love love on!

What do the roses say, dear, my dear,
   Pale and dewy and blood-red all?
Stay me with kisses, the night is anear,
   And the rose leaves fall!

What do the roses say, heart, my heart,
   Proud, impatient, and tossed with doubt?
Bloom and beauty from life may part,
   But life lengthens out!

VISIONS OF THE NIGHT.

O THE visions that the night brings,
O the fluttering of white wings,
O benignant eyes and beautiful that down upon us
    bend !
O the hum of happy voices,
O the glad throng that rejoices,
When the visions of the midnight bring the absent
    friend to friend !

O the dainty feet that find me,
O the dimpled arms that bind me,
Of the little love that softly from the star-land comes
    to me !
O the gladness, past revealing,
Filling soul and heart and feeling,
When upon my yearning bosom she is sleeping
    peacefully !

Ah, how sweet to know this dreaming
Is a glimpse, a twilight gleaming,

Of the beauty and the glory of the heaven we adore ;
    And the faces which behold us,
    And the arms that fondly fold us,
Are the faces and embraces of the loved ones gone
    before.

    O the comfort that the night brings,
    O the fluttering of white wings,
O benignant eyes and beautiful that down upon us
    bend !
    O the hum of happy voices,
    O the glad throng that rejoices,
When the visions of the midnight bring the absent
    friend to friend !

THE FIRST CROCUS.

Do you know where the crocus blows?
Under the snows;
Wide-eyed and winsome and daintily fair
As waxen exotic close-tended and rare;
    Every child knows
    Where the first crocus blows.

Do you know why the crocus grows
Under the snows?
To tell that the winter is over and gone,
And soon bird and blossom will gladden the lawn
    And the hedge-rows
    Where the first crocus blows.

Do you know when the crocus grows
Under the snows?
When little ones sleep in their warm downy beds,
With mother-hands smoothing their dear curly
      heads;
    While the storm goes
    Where the first crocus blows.

Do you know while the crocus grows
Under the snows,
That One smileth softly and says, " I will send
This promise that all stormy times have an end."
So our Lord knows
Where the first crocus blows.

MARION.

OH, have you seen my Marion,
Sweet summer breezes, flying far
From sun to sun, from star to star?
Have ye caressed her soft brown hair,
And kissed her feet and white arms bare?
Then whither, tell me, hath she flown,
My little one, my love, my own—
    My Marion!

My pretty blue-eyed Marion,
Whose small white hands swept o'er my face
With such a dainty, tender grace,
Who slept so softly on my breast,
And woke, a glad bird from her nest;
Bear ye no message, breezes, say,
From her I mourn both night and day—
    My Marion!

Have ye not seen my Marion,
O sunbeams as ye dancing go
From fields of bloom to peaks of snow?

She passed so quickly from my sight,
My poor, sad eyes were dazzled quite,
And but a moment could I see
The white host bearing her from me—
        My Marion !

    O little, loving Marion !
Is it in kingdoms far away
You wait for me both night and day?
Is it in lands beyond the sun,
In groves of spice and cinnamon ?
Is it in gardens glad with bloom,
And redolent with sweet perfume—
        My Marion ?

    Ah, dimpled, darling Marion !
I fain would be the one to meet
Your tiny, tottering, tipsy feet ;
I fain would run with outstretched arms,
To soothe your childish, sweet alarms ;
Would smoothe your skirts and comb your hair,
And rock you in the glad blue air —
        My Marion !

O laughing, lisping Marion !
When I on some autumnal morn
Go through the vales of tasseled corn,
And purpling vines and bending trees,
And singing birds and humming bees,
Shall I not in some secret place
Behold you, darling, face to face—
        My Marion ?

O pure and patient Marion !
Or child, or maid, when all is done,
Your face will be the same sweet one ;
The shy, glad welcome in your eyes,
My dream fulfilled of Paradise !
But now, oh, whither have you flown,
My little one, my love, my own —
        My Marion !

MY NAMESAKE.

WITH the sunshine and the flowers,
With the sweets of summer showers,
With the daisies and the dew,
With the violets so blue;
With the shy forget-me-not
Hiding in sequestered spot;
In the arms of kindly Fate,
Came our darling Baby Kate.

When she came, the Sunshine said:
"I will crown her dainty head
With the finest threads they spin
In the realms Elysian;"
Said the Violets: "Her eyes
Shall reflect our fairest dyes;"
While the Lily and the Rose
On her cheeks and lips repose;
And the Zephyrs dancing wait
On the steps of Baby Kate.

Child of sunshine and of flowers,
Child of sweetest summer showers,
Bud and blossom into bloom,
Fill our lives with glad perfume.
Thou the fairest thing that blows,
Be it lily, be it rose ;
On thy dawning life we wait,
Dainty, darling Baby Kate !

FRATERNITY, CHARITY, LOYALTY.

SEARCH each comrade's heart, and there,
Graven with the tenderest care,
You will find these letters three
Linked in blessed trinity,—
Honored, loved, and heeded well,
Honored more than tongue can tell,—
Golden are they—*F., C., L.*

Great is this Fraternity —
Brooding o'er the flight of years,
Born of love for you and me,
Born of battle and of tears ;
These are they who stood the test
When the charging columns prest—
Won their fame, and are at rest.

Charity ! — a gracious spell
Wrought in days of doom and dread,
When they stooped to hearken well
What a dying comrade said—

For the wives and orphans far,
Shivering in the blasts of war;
For the shattered ones that are.

Loyalty ! — 'twas theirs to show
What are faith and fealty,
Upward where the bugles blow
On the heights of Victory;
Upward from the gloom of night,
From the clamor of the fight,
To the blaze of Freedom's light.

Comrades — ye whose hearts are sealed
To the glorious trinity —
We our reverent homage yield,
Lift the hat and bend the knee !
Honor to whom honor's due,
Honor to the loyal Blue,—
Honor, love, from me and you !

THE POET'S WORLD.

THE poet rose, his heart was light,
  He journeyed with the sun ;
He blessed the golden day ; at night
  He hailed the dark begun ;
Because, you see, his heart was light —
  His life was in its sun.

The poet said : "A fairer world
  Lies just beyond my ken ;
Methinks I see its flags unfurled,
  Its royal ranks of men."
His hope it was the poet's world,
  His sight the poet's ken.

But when long days he walked alone,
  And saw the world the same —
But that the hills were higher grown,
  And that his feet were lame,—
He wondered : "Is the world so lone,
  Or is my heart the same ?"

And so he sat him down and wept,
  His days they were so sad,
And wondered if the friends he left
  Were feeling quite as bad ; —
You see, the poet when he wept
  Thought all the world was sad.

And then the poet turned him round,
  And vowed no more to roam ;
No fairer country had he found
  Than that he left at home, —
As things will ever come around
  To those who vow to roam.

The poet's heart is mine to-day ;
  And thus it is I know
There are no happier scenes than lay
  Around the Long Ago ;
The poet's heart mine own to-day,
  This truth I feel and know.

No friends so true, no eyes so kind,
  No life so sweet and fair,
As in the days we left behind,
  The days so free from care ;

The fealty and the faith so kind,
  The life so wondrous fair.

Heaven rest the poet's faithful heart,
  Heaven rest his soul and mine,
And give us all when far apart
  This comfort all divine :
That Heaven will rest the faithful heart,
  This soul of mine and thine!

HE LEADETH ME.

Not always through the meadows fair and wide,
  In peaceful valley and by sunlit sea,
Not always where the quiet waters glide,
  He leadeth me.

Nay, oft the paths are perilous and steep;
  Nay, oft below the waves beat angrily;
Nay, oft through shadows where I pausing weep
  He leadeth me.

Once, all the days in merriment went by,
  And all the nights in idle revelry;
I lived to laugh, and, laughing, mocked the cry—
  " He leadeth me ! "

" O sweet, sweet wealth of life ! " I woke to say,
  And bound my girdle for the rounds of glee;
And would not heed Him pleading in the way,
  Who leadeth me.

The morning shadows fled across the plain,
   The noontide burned, my feet sank wearily;
He turned and left me blinded in my pain,
     Who leadeth me.

All day upon the withered earth I lay,—
   O cruel Earth, that erst so kind could be!—
And scarce I heard the whispered message say,
     "He leadeth me."

All day the sun consumed me with his flame,—
   O hateful sun, once beautiful to see!—
Upon my burning brow the impress came:
     "He leadeth me."

I saw it on the grasses bowed and bent,
   And in the lightnings flashing angrily,
And on the storm-clouds black and thunder-rent:
     "He leadeth me."

"O thou Supreme!" I said, "on sea and land,
   Whose mighty face for shame I may not see,
Vouchsafe but this: one pressure of the hand
     That leadeth me!"

And softly through the gloom it clasped my own,
   And raised me gently to my bended knee;
I rose, and saw the halo from Him thrown,
      Who leadeth me.

And now, though in the desert waste I go,
   Or through the storm, or on the pitiless sea,
I fear nor foe nor pain; for well I know
      He leadeth me.

And so I feel, my trembling hand in His,
   It is but well where'er my life may be;
If present glories fade, to greater bliss
      He leadeth me.

"AUF WIEDERSEHEN."

NAY, not good-bye ! a kindlier word
Our Teuton cousinship has stirred,
To give a hope for parting days
To him who goes, to him who stays,—
The hope that we may meet again :
Auf wiedersehen ! Auf wiedersehen !

And so we speed thee, parting friend,
And forth to fame and fortune send ;
And though we pray that you may find
As faithful friends as those behind,
Yet still in joy or still in pain :
Auf wiedersehen ! Auf wiedersehen !

And should the great world prove unkind,
And fame and fortune hard to find ;
Should sorrow come, or friends forsake,
And discipline be hard to take,
Retrace your steps, the way is plain :
Auf wiedersehen ! Auf wiedersehen !

Important Books Selected

FROM THE PUBLICATIONS
OF

Jansen, McClurg, & Co.

ARNOLD (Hon. Isaac N.) — **Life of Abraham Lincoln.** 8vo, gilt top, 471 pages, with steel portrait. Price, $2.50.

"The details of the life of self-made 'Honest Abe' read like a romance, and are woven together with a deftness that gives the work a rare fascination." —*Cincinnati Enquirer.*

"It is the only life of Lincoln thus far published that is likely to live, the only one that has any serious pretensions to depict him with adequate veracity, completeness, and dignity."—*New York Sun.*

"Mr. Arnold succeeded to a singular extent in assuming the broad view and judicious voice of posterity and exhibiting the greatest figure of our time in its true perspective."—*New York Tribune.*

BALDWIN (James, Ph.D.) — **The Book-Lover.** A Guide to the Best Reading. 16mo, gilt top, 202 pages. Price, $1.25.

"Compact with suggestions and wisdom."—*N. Y. Mail and Express.*

"Crowded with thought and valuable information. * * * It is a practical answer to the question, 'What shall I read?'"—*Cincinnati Commercial Gazette.*

BROWNE (Francis F.) — **Golden Poems** by British and American Authors. Edited by Francis F. Browne. Crown 8vo, full gilt, 464 pages. Price, $2.00.

"A book to delight the eye and warm the heart and strengthen the intellect. This large, handsomely bound volume contains a larger amount of true poetic thought than we have ever seen gathered together in equal compass."—*Boston Golden Rule.*

CARPENTER (Frank D. Y.) — **Round About Rio.** Descriptions of the Brazilian Capital and vicinity. Price, $1.50.

"A bright and interesting book, which may be read as a record of travel, and read at the same time as a realistic novel."—*N. Y. Mail and Express.*

"A book which the thoughtful will read for information, and the young for its genuine fun."—*N. Y. Christian Advocate.*

COX (Rev. G. W)—**Tales of Ancient Greece.** 12mo, 372 pages. Price, $1.50.

"Admirable in style, and level with a child's comprehension. These versions might well find a place in every family."—*The Nation.*

CUMNOCK (R. McL.)—**Choice Readings** for Public and Private Entertainment. Arranged for the Exercises of the School, College and Public Reader, with Elocutionary Advice. Large 12mo, 478 pages. Price, $1.75.

"Among the multitude of books issued for the same purpose during the past ten years, we know of none so complete in all respects, and so well fitted to the needs of the elocutionist as the volume before us."—*Boston Transcript.*

FAY (Amy)—**Music-Study in Germany.** 12mo, 352 pages. Price, $1.25.

" They are charming letters, both in style and matter, and the descriptions of Tausig, Kullak, Liszt and Deppe, with each of whom Miss Fay studied, are done with all the delicacy of a sketch by Meissonier."—*Boston Globe.*

JULIAN (Hon. Geo. W.)—**Political Recollections** from 1840 to 1872. 12mo, 384 pages. Price, $1.50.

" The production of a man who may look back upon a public career, of which, in point of character and devotion to a principle, anybody might be very proud."—*Atlantic Monthly.*

" The author's attitude is that of one who is done with politics and can review the fields fought over generally without bitterness."—*New York Sun.*

KIRKLAND (Miss E. S.)—**A Short History of France,** for Young People. 12mo, 398 pages. Price, $1.50.

"Both instructive and entertaining. It is not a dry compendium of dates and facts, but a charmingly written history."—*Christian Union.*

KIRKLAND (Miss E. S.)—**Speech and Manners** for Home and School. Square 12mo, 263 pages. Price, $1.00.

" The authors theory of manners and of speech is good. Her modest manual might be read, re-read and read again with great advantage in most American families."—*New York Independent.*

LINN (Rev. S. P.)—**Golden Thoughts.** From the Words of leading Orators, Divines, Philosophers, Statesmen and Poets. Crown 8vo, 448 pages, full gilt.   Price, $2.00.

"Veritable gems of thought, couched in the best English phraseology." —*Cincinnati Times-Star.*

"It is the choice fruit of the finest intellects. And through the whole these intellectual suns sparkle, and glow, and beam."—*Boston Golden Rule.*

NOHL (Dr. Louis)—**Biographies of Musicians**—MOZART; BEETHOVEN; HAYDN; WAGNER; LISZT. Translated from the German by G. P. Upton. 12mo, with portrait.   Price per volume, $1.25.   *The five volumes in neat box,* $6.25.

LIFE OF MOZART.—" He lives in these pages as the world saw him, from his marvelous boyhood till his untimely death."—*Standard.*

LIFE OF BEETHOVEN.—" It will be welcomed by all lovers of music as a strong, firm picture of the great composer, and a record of the incidents of his life."—*The Alliance.*

LIFE OF HAYDN.—"No fuller history of his career, the society in which he moved, and of his personal life can be found than is given in this work."—*Boston Gazette.*

LIFE OF WAGNER.—"Herr Nohl's biography is terse, concise, enthusiastic, and at the same time just."—*Philadelphia Press.*

LIFE OF LISZT.—" It is the biography of a musician who was doubtless divinely endowed with a musical faculty rarely paralleled in any age."—*New York Christian Advocate.*

RICHARDSON (Abby Sage)—**Familiar Talks on English Literature.** A Manual embracing the Great Epochs of English Literature, from the conquest of Britain, 449, to the death of Scott, 1832. 12mo, 454 pages.   Price, $1.75.

" The work is, without question, one of the best of the kind with which we are acquainted ; if for no other reason, because it has in greater measure than usual the capacity to interest the young readers, for whom it is intended."—*New York Evening Post.*

ROBINSON (S. T.)—**The Shadow of the War.** A story of Reconstruction Times. 12mo, 378 pages.   Price, $1.25.

" The story has strength and point, freshness of material, self-evident naturalness and truthfulness, and the interest of an eye-witness' picture of memorable times."—*Literary World.*

TOPELIUS (Z.)—**The Surgeon's Stories.**   Translated from the original Swedish, and comprising : TIMES OF GUS- TAF ADOLF ; TIMES OF BATTLE AND REST ; TIMES OF CHARLES XII ; TIMES OF FREDERICK I ; TIMES OF LINNÆUS ; TIMES OF ALCHEMY. Each book is complete in itself, but an historical sequence and unity connect the series.   Price per volume, $1.25.   *The six volumes in box*, $7.50.

TIMES OF GUSTAF ADOLF.—"' The Story of the Thirty Years War ' is a fascinating chapter in history, and Topelius writes of it with great imaginative powers and charm of style."—*Boston Journal of Education.*

TIMES OF BATTLE AND REST.—" The admirer of lofty romance cannot fail to be grateful for an introduction through this careful and spirited English version to the Scandinavian Scott."—*New York Independent.*

TIMES OF CHARLES XII.—" Full of dramatic power, and thrilling with incidents of war, adventure, and love. The picture drawn of Charles XII is a strong one, and better than any historic narrative."—*Boston Christian Register.*

TIMES OF FREDERICK I. — " With each volume we congratulate ourselves upon the opportunity afforded of thoroughly understanding the history and times of Sweden and countries connected. The style is so en- grossing that one cannot bear to lay the book down until every page has been read."—*Pittsburgh Chronicle-Telegraph.*

TIMES OF LINNÆUS.—" Like its predecessor in the series, the story is abundant in spirit, movement, and incidents, while the recital is character- ized by fire, picturesqueness, and force."—*Boston Gazette.*

TIMES OF ALCHEMY.—" This volume completes a charming series of stories, possessing not merely fine fancy, but having within them such faithful pictures of Northern European life as can be found in no other books." —*N. W. Christian Advocate.*

WHEELER (Ella) — **Maurine and Other Poems.** 12mo, 254 pages.   Price, $1.50.

" Few female poetical writers are better known throughout the United States than Miss Wheeler, or more deservedly admired. The volume contains a number of poems that are given to the public for the first time, among which ' Maurine' stands out boldly, for originality of thought, power of ex- pression, and characteristic literary merit."—*Philadelphia Sun.*

Any of the books on this list sent by mail, post paid, on receipt of price, by the publishers,

JANSEN, McCLURG, & CO., Chicago.